To: Larry & Jill

Thanks For Your Support

May You Be Blessed

Sieu Rambhajan

Trinidad and Tobago

Terrific and Tranquil

HANSIB

First published in 2000 by Hansib Publications Limited
Tower House, 141-149 Fonthill Road, London N4 3HF, England

ISBN 1 870518 67 5

Production by Hansib Publications Ltd, London

Origination by Graphic Ideas Studios, London

Printed and bound in Britain by Caledonian International Book Manufacturing, Glasgow

Foreword

THERE has never been a better time to produce a book on Trinidad and Tobago - this rainbow nation and land of the hummingbird.

Blessed with a dynamic, industrious, multi-racial people, uniquely rich culture, advantageous location, abundant natural resources, and spectacular and unspoiled scenery and nature, the country can self-confidently stride into the next millennium with a better quality of life for all its people.

The Hansib 'Nations' series has itself been a uniquely successful project. I am quite confident that this latest volume will join that proud tradition. With its one people of African, Indian, Chinese, Arab, European and other origins, Trinidad and Tobago must be the most harmoniously diverse group of 1.3 million people under heaven. Indeed, were it not for the fact that our book on India was titled *A Wealth of Diversity*, I feel that the twin-island Caribbean republic would surely have merited this designation.

I was first inspired to produce a book on the Republic of Trinidad and Tobago back in 1990, almost a decade ago, when the then Prime Minister, A.N.R. Robinson, and I discussed it with his Ambassador, Edwin Carrington. Sadly, an outbreak of political turmoil meant that the project could not be realised at that point. Despite a number of attempts to get things moving again, it was only when Basdeo Panday became Prime Minister that things really took off from our discussions in late 1998. Prime Minister Panday introduced me to Vishnu Ramlogan of TIDCO, and the result is in your hands.

Trinidad and Tobago, of course, still has a journey to travel and has wisely chosen to prioritise both inward investment and eco-tourism. No visitor to the country can fail to be impressed by the genuine effort being made by all stake-holders in its society to bring people and communities together and to go forward in harmony.

In the words of Prime Minister Basdeo Panday, "Let us continue to work together to build a land where our children will be protected. Where our women will be respected. The land where every citizen will be saved. A land of increasing prosperity in which every citizen will enjoy equal opportunity for a better life."

And in a world still too frequently scarred by ethnic hatreds and divisions, let us pay homage to where the Ganges meets the Nile!

Arif Ali
December 1999

Acknowledgements

In the pages of this book you will find an attempt to evoke the spirit of Trinidad and Tobago - its natural beauty and the genius of its people. In any country, the people are, and make, the nation - and nowhere is this more true than in the twin-island Land of the Hummingbird.

Like all Caribbean peoples, the sons and daughters of this nation are scattered far and wide. But they are all ambassadors for a land they never forget.

Let me pay tribute, therefore, to those outstanding Trinidadians and Tobagonians - men and women of the calibre of Pearl Connor, Rudy Walker, Nina Baden-Semper, Brian Lara, Sonny Ramadin, Sir Trevor McDonald, Dwight Yorke, Ron Ramdin, the late CLR James, and the late Claudia Jones to name a few. A number of them have been my friends and colleagues for years. All of them have inspired and guided me and countless others in ways too numerous to mention. In a very real sense, this book is for them and of them. To all of them, I extent my grateful thanks and my intellectual debt. *AA*

Special thanks to: Kash Ali, who has served throughout as the indispensable and unflappable co-ordinator and managing editor of a project with deadlines that only I would dare to impose, and to my colleague, Isha Persaud.

Grateful thanks to: *The photographers*, Bruce Anton, who assisted with the photo editing, Farouk Khan, Junia Browne, Kenneth Lee, Molly Gaskin, Noel Norton, Richard Cook, Shirley Bahadur, Stephen Broadbridge, Allsport, and the Ministry of Information, Communications, Training and Distance Learning, and *the writers*, Jalaludin Khan, Burton Sankeralli, Tony Deyal, Terry Joseph, Raymond Ramcharitar, Simon Lee, Rajandaye Ramkissoon-Chen, Kris Rampersad, Annabelle Ove, Lucretia Gabriel, Michelle Lewis, Dr Austin Trinidade, Vaneisa Baksh, Peter Hannomansingh, Mervyn Crichlow, Angela Gouveia.

And thanks to: Lucy Ali, Paul Fraser, Shareef Ali, Richard Painter, Alan Cross, Ella Barnes, Alissia Barrow, Boyer Jaggassar, Camellia Neptune, Candyce M Kelshall, Carlos John, Charlie Ramsumair, Christine Taylor, Dennis Romany, Donald Baldeosingh, Ernistine Pearce, Errol Hosein, Fidel Persaud, Gideon Maxime, Derek Alan-Noel Parker, Glen Cunin, Heika Smith, Hermus Dowers, Indra Kanhai, Indrani Deyal, Jane Watkins, Judith Laird, Kathleen Pinder, J. Williams Schmidhammer, Lala Kanhai, Lana De Gannes, Mary Norton, Aliza Ali, Maureen Lawrence, Mervyn Assam, Mervyn Grant, Nylah Juman, Peter Kanhai, Renate Schnabel, Sandra Chouti, Keith Bennett, Pope Seemungal, Ramjohn Ali, Relindor Kanhai, Indira Maharaj, Bonnie Khan, Richard Ramdial, Roger St Bernard, Sat Balkaransingh, Raffique Shah, Shareef Juman, Sheelagh M De Osuna, Sharrell Duff, Stephen Webster, Teresa White, Willie Chen, Dr Wilfred Chen, Dr Raj Chen, Dr Tim Gopeesingh, Victor Maloney, Vinood Narwani, Vishnu Ramlogan, Zorida Kanhai, Kelly-Anne Balfour, Heather Gabriel, Dr Carla Noel, Ian Ali, Norman Aleong, Wilfred Naimool, Remasis Information Services Limited, and the Tourism and Industrial Development Company (TIDCO).

We would like to thank the following individuals, companies and organisations for their help and support: Airport Authority of Trinidad and Tobago, Angostura Limited, Ansa McAL Limited, Association of Caribbean States, Blue Horizon Resort, British Gas Trinidad and Tobago Limited, Carib Brewery, Caroni (1975) Limited, CBP Holdings, Chief Brand Products, CL Financial Limited, Dr Deo Singh, Embassy of the Federative Republic of Brazil, Global Friendship Forum, Trinmar, Grafton Beach Resort, Guardian Life of the Caribbean Limited, Hi-Lo Food Stores, Le Gran Courlan Resort and Spa, M.I. Juman & Sons Limited, Mecalfab Limited, Metropolitan Book Suppliers, Mico Garment Factory Limited, Ministry of Tobago Affairs, Misons Industries Limited, N.E.M. (West Indies) Insurance Limited, Neil & Massy Motors, Northern Construction Limited, Petroleum Company of Trinidad and Tobago Limited (Petrotrin), Point Lisas Industrial Port Development Corporation Limited (PLIPDECO), Port Authority of Trinidad and Tobago, Printex Converters, Telecommunications Services of Trinidad and Tobago Limited (TSTT), The Co-operative Citrus Growers' Association of Trinidad and Tobago, The National Gas Company of Trinidad and Tobago Limited, The National Library and Information System Authority, The Normandie Hotel, The Royal Bank of Trinidad and Tobago Limited, Titan Methanol Company, Tobago Plantations Limited, Trinidad and Tobago Manufacturers' Association, Trinidad and Tobago Sightseeing Tours. Our apologies to those we have inadvertently omitted.

The Republic of Trinidad and Tobago

Coat of Arms

The Coat of Arms of Trinidad and Tobago was designed in 1962 by a committee of distinguished citizens established to select and design the country's national emblems. Committee members included noted artist Carlyle Chang and carnival designer George Bailey. The Coat of Arms incorporates important historical and indigenous elements of Trinidad and Tobago. They are: The shield, the Helm of special design, the Mantle which covers the Helm, the Wreath to hold the Mantle in place, the Crest, the Supporters and the Motto.

At the top is the Crest - a ship's wheel in gold in front of a fruited coconut palm. This palm had always been the central figure on the Great Seals of British Colonial Tobago. Beneath the wheel is the wreath which holds the mantle in place.

The Helm is a gold helmet facing front which represents the Queen. The devices on the Shield are the humming birds. The three gold ships represent the Trinity - the discovery of the islands and the three ships of Columbus; the sea that brought our people together; and the commerce and wealth of the country. The colours of the National Flag's are displayed on the Shield.

The Supporters are a scarlet ibis (the national bird of Trinidad) on the left and a cocrico (the national bird of Tobago) on the right. Both are shown in their natural colours. The Three Peaks may have been chosen to commemorate Columbus's decision to name Trinidad after the Blessed Trinity or the same three peaks called the "Three Sisters" which a sailor on Columbus's ship saw rising from the south of the island. Inscribed on the motto scroll are the words: "Together we aspire; together we achieve".

The National Flag

J. BROWNE

The National Flag was selected from a series of designs created by the Independence Committee in 1962. The colours of red, white and black were chosen to reflect the philosophy of the 'new nation', the principles for which it stood, its hopes and aspirations and the nation's supreme determination to preserve the harmony and unity of spirit which underlie the cultural diversity of its people. These colours also represent the elements of Earth, Water and Fire which are embodied in the nation's past, present and future.

Black represents the dedication of the people joined together by one strong bond. It is the colour of strength, of unity of purpose, and

Chaconia

Scarlet ibis

Cocrico

of the wealth of the land; Red represents fire. It is the colour most expressive of the nation; the vitality of the land and its peoples; the warmth and energy of the sun, the courage and friendliness of the people; White is the sea by which the land is bound; the cradle of the nation's heritage; the purity of aspirations and the equality of all people under the sun.

The National Flower

The National Flower - the chaconia - also called 'wild poinsettia', is a flaming red forest flower. Belonging to the family *rubiaceae*, this flower owes its botanical name *warszewiczia coccinea* to the Polish-Lithuanian plant collector, Joseph Warszewicz. The name 'chaconia' was given in honour of the last and most progressive Spanish Governor of Trinidad, Don Jose Maria Chacon. This flower, recognised by its long sprays of magnificent vermilion, usually blooms around the time of the nation's Anniversary of Independence, 31 August. The colour of this bloom echoes the symbolism of the colour red in the national flag and on the shield of the Coat Of Arms.

The National Birds

The National Birds of Trinidad and Tobago are the scarlet ibis (Trinidad) and the cocrico (Tobago). Both are protected by law.

The largest habitat of the scarlet ibis is the Caroni Swamp in central Trinidad. The cocrico is native to both Tobago and Venezuela and is commonly referred to as the Tobago pheasant.

National Awards

Since independence on 31 August 1962, Trinidad and Tobago has honoured outstanding and deserving service. These awards are given on the anniversary of independence.

The Trinity Cross is the highest award that a citizen can receive and it is given to persons or groups that have rendered distinguished and outstanding service to Trinidad and Tobago. *The Humming Bird Medal* is given to people who have rendered long and devoted service in the field of labour, sports and culture. It is awarded in gold, silver or bronze. *The Chaconia Medal* is given to people who have rendered long and meritorious service in the field of community work and social welfare. It is awarded in gold, silver or bronze. *The Public Service Medal of Merit* is given to members in the public service for outstanding and meritorious service. It is awarded in gold, silver or bronze.

THE NATIONAL ANTHEM

Forged from the love of liberty,
In the fires of hope and prayer,
With boundless faith in our Destiny,
We solemnly declare.

Side by side we stand,
Islands of the blue Caribbean Sea,
This our Native Land,
We pledge our lives the Thee.

Here every creed and race find an equal place,
And may God bless our Nation,
Here every creed and race find an equal place,
And may God bless our Nation.

Contents

MINISTRY OF INFORMATION

President, A.N.R. Robinson

MINISTRY OF INFORMATION

Prime Minister, Basdeo Panday

Above right - Emperor Haile Selassie of Ethiopia arriving at Piarco Airport. Dr Eric Williams, left, introduces the Emperor to the then Finance Minister, A.N.R. Robinson

Opposite page
Top - Queen Elizabeth II completes the signing of the visitors' book at the town hall in Port of Spain in 1966. Officiating the ceremony is Eddie Taylor, Mayor of Port of Spain. The Queen is accompanied by the Duke of Edinburgh

Bottom - Official visit of Queen Elizabeth II and the Duke of Edinburgh, 1958

rest held back for nomination by the Governor or reserved for senior civil servants), this limited form of democracy was, nevertheless, the first step towards independence.

The 1956 elections saw the rise of a new, vehemently nationalistic political party led by Dr Eric Williams. The People's National Movement (PNM) won thirteen of the twenty four seats and became the first Party government in Trinidad and Tobago. The PNM was victorious again in the 1961 elections, winning twenty of the thirty available seats, and the Party now set its sights, firmly, on independence from Britain. The following year, on 31 August 1962, Trinidad and Tobago achieved independence.

The PNM remained in power for an unprecedented thirty years, during which time the nation finally severed the last ties with the British Crown and became a Republic on 1 August 1976.

Long-term office has its set-backs and the PNM has had its share of crises. In 1970, the Black Power movement and the labour unions were clamouring for social change. At the same time, a faction within the army attempted a military coup. The political unrest was resolved by the Williams government, which imposed a state of emergency until calm was restored. A second aggressive incident once again challenged the nation's leaders - this time the Government of the day was the National Alliance for Reconstruction (NAR). On 27 July 1990, an armed group, who were members of the Islamic Jamaat al Muslimeen community, stormed the Parliament building and took the Prime Minister hostage along with members of his government and the opposition. The stand-off lasted five days, by which time an amnesty had been negotiated and the hostages released.

The NAR Government survived for just one term in office and were defeated in the 1991 General Election by a resurgent PNM. However, an early election called in November 1995, resulted in an historic stalemate. The two major parties - the United National Congress (UNC) and the PNM - each won seventeen seats, with the NAR holding on to the two seats in Tobago. The deadlock was resolved when a coalition was agreed between the NAR and the UNC, led by Basdeo Panday who became the nation's new Prime Minister.

N. NORTON

N. NORTON

MINISTRY OF INFORMATION

Patrick Manning

MINISTRY OF INFORMATION

Noor Hassanali

N. NORTON

Sir Solomon Hochoy, first locally elected Governor and first local President

N. NORTON

Bishop Desmond Tutu addresses thousands at the National Stadium

Right - Officials attend the 45th Commonwealth Parliamentary Conference

S. BAHADUR

Miss Trinidad and Tobago, Wendy Fitzwilliams, receives a hero's welcome at the Queen's Park Oval after winning Miss Universe 1998

N. NORTON

B. ANTON

Right, from top
Anglican Church in Rio Claro

Barrackpore mosque

Paschi Kashim mandir in St James

J. BROWNE

J. BROWNE

F. KHAN

Opposite page
Top - Hindu wedding in Chaguanas
Bottom - Muslim prayers during Eid

Previous page
St Michael's Roman Catholic Church in the Maracas Valley

R. COOK

F. KHAN

F. KHAN

Statue of the Hindu god, Shiva, in the 'Temple on the Sea'

J. BROWNE

F. KHAN

Above right, down
Entrance to Hindu temple in Piparo

Mosque on Queen Street in Port of Spain

Mandir on Ethel Street in St James

F. KHAN

Opposite page
Hindu mandir on in San Fernanado

F. KHAN

B. ANTON

Above - Roman Catholic Church in St Joseph, the former capital of Trinidad and Tobago

Right - Hindu temple in Piparo

J. BROWNE

Opposite page
Top - Rio Claro Roman Catholic church
Bottom - The shrine at St Ann's Catholic Church in Port of Spain

Page 28
Top - Hindu Puja
Bottom - The Seminary at Mount St Benedict

Page 29
Statue of Christ at Quesnel's House in the Maracas Valley

F. KHAN

F. KHAN

J. BROWNE

B. ANTON

B. ANTON

J. BROWNE

F. KHAN

N. NORTON

S. BROADBRIDGE

The faces of Trinidad and Tobago

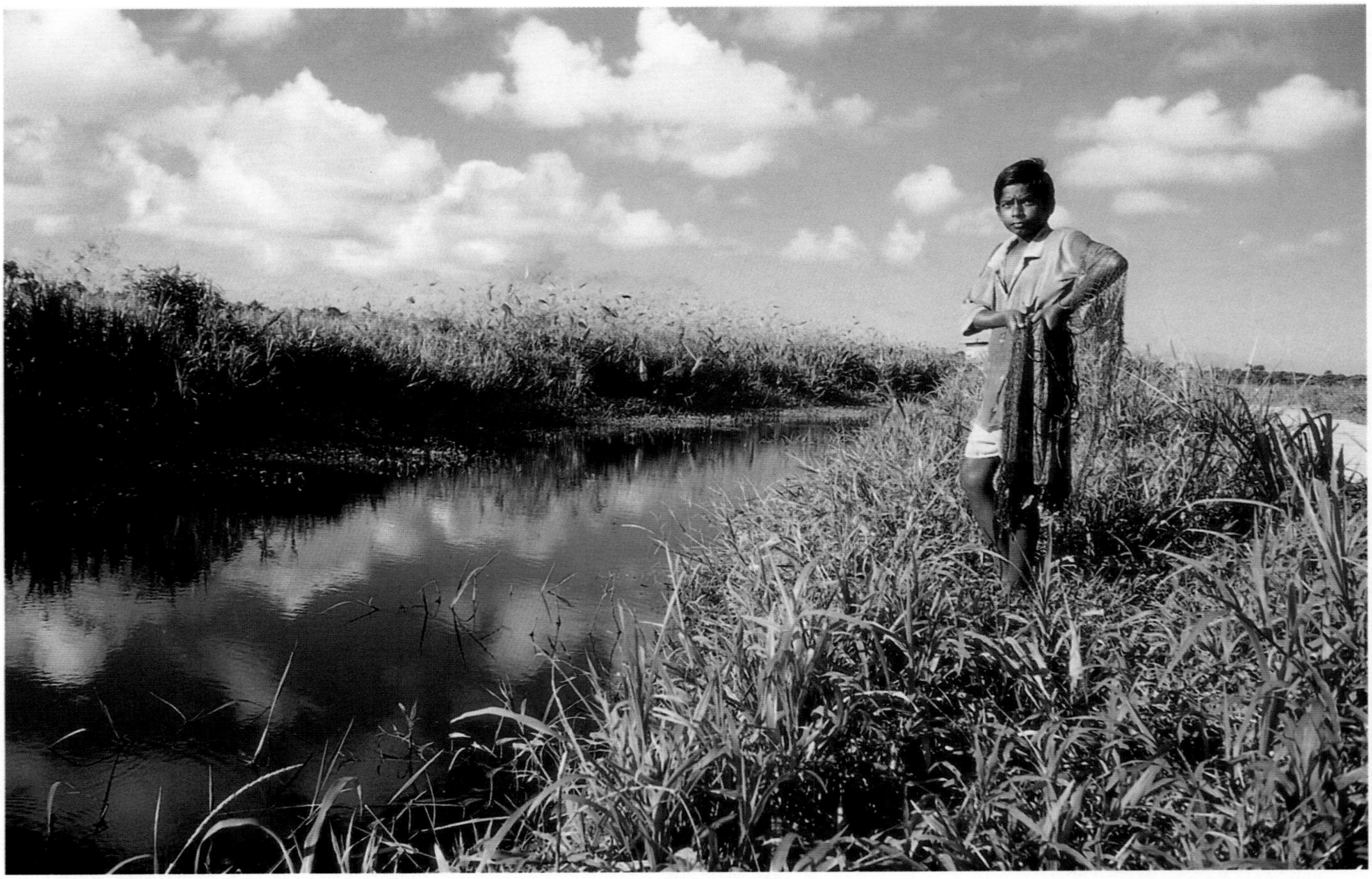
S. BROADBRIDGE

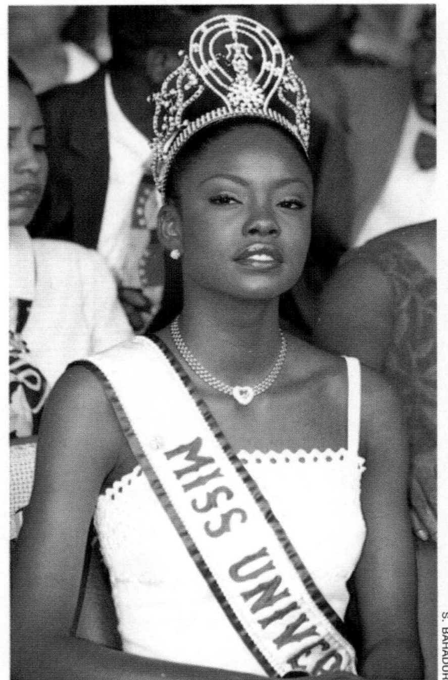

MISS UNIVE
S. BAHADUR

Wendy Fitzwilliams, Miss Trinidad and Tobago and Miss Universe 1998

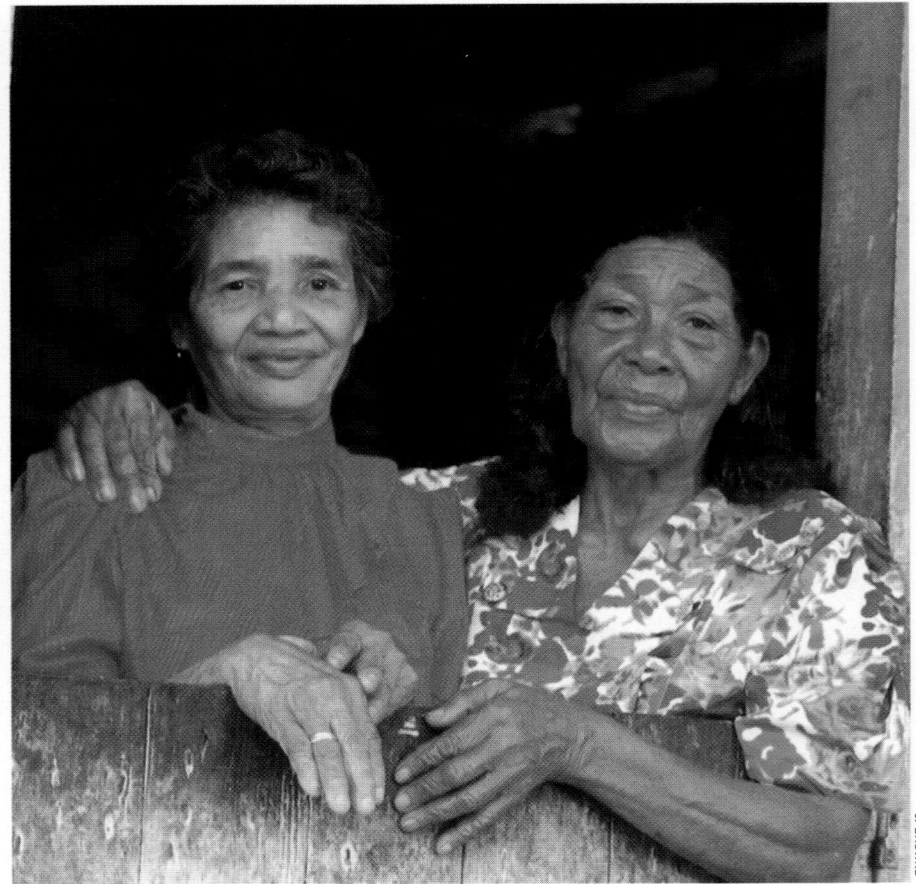

J. BROWNE

Right - Amerindian sisters

F. KHAN

J. BROWNE

R. COOK

M. GASKIN

J. BROWNE

J. BROWNE

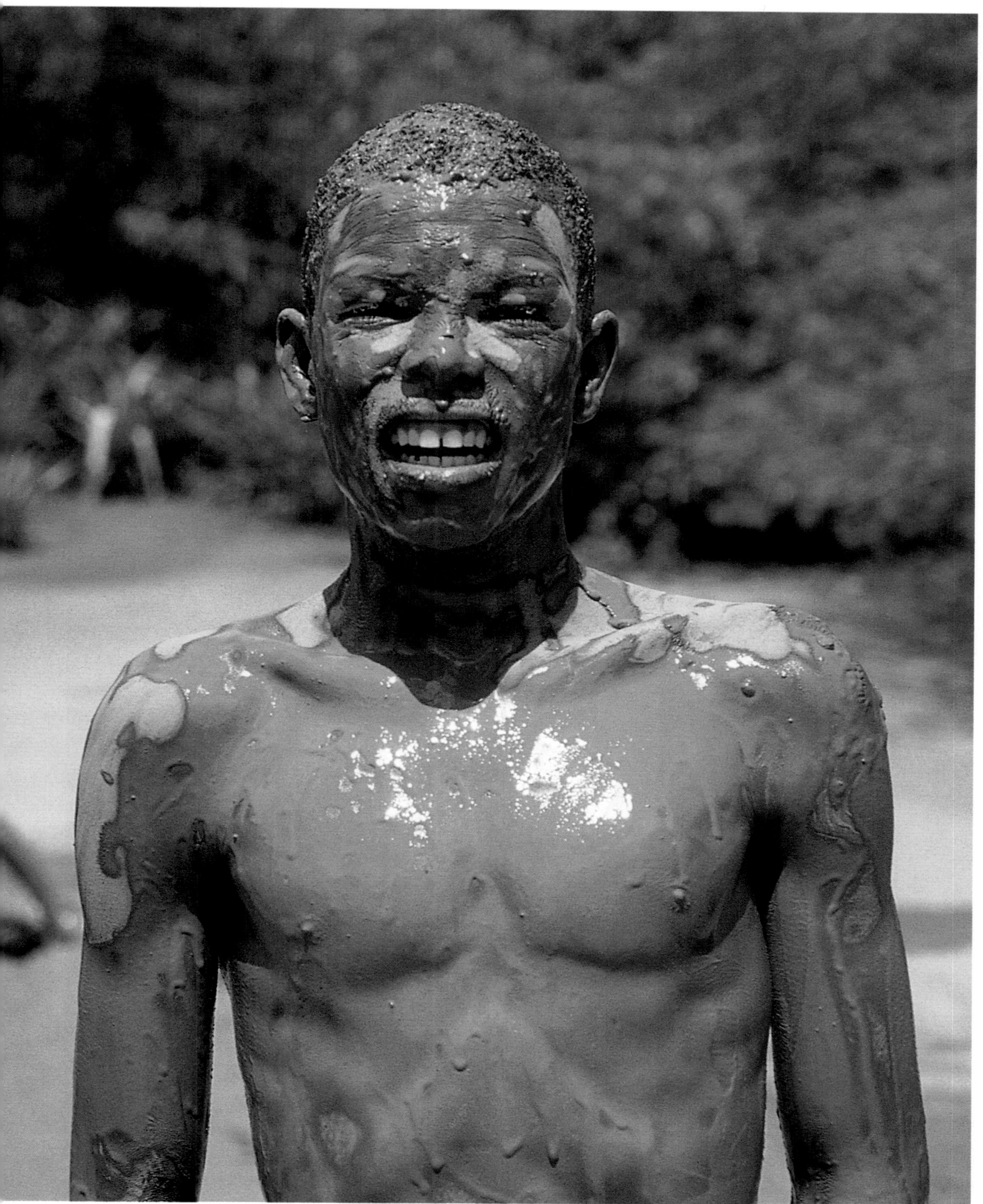

J. BROWNE

R. COOK

A brotherhood bound by the sound of drums

Terry Joseph

THE annual Shiite Muslim commemoration of the deeply significant martyrdom of Imam Hussain, takes the form of solemn processions for three successive nights and the afternoon of the fourth day, fuelled by the rhythms of infectious drumming on the one hand and undying faith on the other.

Observed in Trinidad since 1846, when the first tadjah appeared on the streets of Phillipine Village, the commemoration is no longer exclusive to devotees of the Shiite persuasion, but has evolved into community efforts, the largest and most spectacular manifestation of which takes place in the village of St James.

It is not uncommon to find Roman Catholics, Hindus, Orishas and members of other faiths working side by side with Muslims to construct the huge replicas of the Imam's tomb, or standing shoulder to shoulder, beating out the rhythms in the tassa bands that accompany the procession. Workers all observe the ten-day fast that begins with the month of Muharram, which marks the beginning of the Islamic lunar calendar.

Fasting and prayers, beginning on the first day of Moharram, accompany the preparation of the tadjahs and drums that form the centre-piece of the street processions that take place on the eighth, ninth and tenth nights and then during sunlight on the following day, which is called Ashura. At sunset on Ashura night (the day previous), the fast is broken and the most spectacular night of the commemoration takes to the streets.

Known locally as 'Hosay' (a corruption of Imam Hussain's name), the street processions attract tens of thousands of spectators each year, as devotees act out four significant events that took place at the Battle of Kerbala in the year 640 AD.

A grandson of Prophet Mohammed, the Imam had sought to defend Islam to the point of war. Mustering a pitifully small group of supporters, the Imam and his seventy-two followers (which included women and children) were slaughtered on the banks of the Euphrates River by the one thousand-man army of the tyrant Yazeed, who had first put them under a three-day siege.

The plight of Abbas, one of the Imam's soldiers, who met his death while attempting to fetch water for children dying of thirst (although he was carrying a white flag as a signal that he was not on a warring mission), is recounted on Flag Night. Devotees carry flags to signify that, if they were at Kerbala, they would have picked up the flag that fell from Abbas.

Opposite page
A young tassa drummer

J. BROWNE

The slaying of defenceless children and the killing of Imam Hussain himself are portrayed in replicas of tombs in the small and large Hosay processions that take place on the second and third nights. On the third night, the 'moons' appear. Gory tales explain the presence of these two half-moons. Tradition has it that one is coloured green because that is the colour that the moon turned on the night that Imam Hussain's brother, Hassan, was poisoned. The red moon is a grim reminder that the head of the Imam was displayed on a pole after the war came to a grisly end. The moons precede the big tadjahs in a grand procession that begins at about 11 p.m. and frequently takes until dawn to cover the three mile route.

The final night sees the only nocturnal appearance of the three dimensional half-moons that "kiss" at about 1 a.m., after being taken to each of the huge tadjahs (known as 'Big Hosay') in a touching ritual. The extraordinarily heavy moons are built on poles which are anchored in holsters at the waist and carried on the shoulders of specially selected men, who do a twirling dance - each carrier only being able to bear the tremendous weight for just a few minutes at a time - before being relieved.

Meanwhile, distinctly beautiful tadjahs, each of which measures up to twenty feet from wheel-base to the top of its perfectly sculptured minaret, seek to rival the Taj Mahal for intricacy and Las Vegas for glitter. They are pulled slowly along the roadway, followed by women who are often moved to tears by the memory of the martyrdom. Many throw rice and coins onto the 'tomb', to ensure that the Imam's spirit is supplied with both food and the wherewithal for his journey. In Middle-Eastern countries and Pakistan, this empathy is sometimes taken to the point of self-flagellation.

The big tadjahs feature colourful and ornate work, painstakingly executed in tin-foil and paper on sculpted, Styrofoam structures. Thousands of little handmade flowers (called 'pan') are stuck along each column (or 'ghumaj'), completely covering the vertical structures. Each of the big tadjahs is accompanied by a tassa-band, which swells to its largest on the final night of the commemoration. The tadjahs, moons and drums come out again on the following day for a parade in the sunlight.

The tassa bands on the final night could feature, at any one time, up to twelve dhol (bass drums), four jhanj (cymbals) and fifteen tassa drummers. In full flight, a tassa band could be heard for miles. Each band plays various rhythms (called 'hands'), as the procession of tadjahs and the piety of the devout seek to recreate the mood that must have prevailed along the route that the martyr's funeral took more than 1,350 years ago in Kerbala, Iraq.

The rhythms in the tassa band range from lively to morose, with the funeral (or 'dead') hand being beaten as a slow, rolling drone, while the war-hand takes on a fiery tempo. The lead beater, known as the cutter, directs the group and takes the initiative in punctuating the rhythm, while the other drummers maintain a steady roll on the tassa behind his customised counterpoint.

The cost of production of the tadjahs, bands and moons are primarily borne by family commitment, although small donations come from sponsors sympathetic to the cause.

Through the years, the commemoration has been subjected to major struggles. An ordinance passed in July 1884 banned Hosay from public roads. Curiously, a Hindu leader quickly drew up a petition

J. BROWNE

R. COOK

Warming the tassa drums for the Hosay celebrations in St James

demanding that the ban be lifted. It was ignored and he and several followers decided to physically resist the legislation by carrying aloft a small tadjah into the streets of San Fernando.

The government of the day ordered police in Port of Spain, Couva and St Joseph to stand ready to join fellow officers in San Fernando to rout the small group. A British warship, the *HMS Dido*, also left the Port of Spain harbour and journeyed to San Fernando to join forces with the local constabulary in the fight against the religious procession.

On 30 October 1884, Arthur Child, a Justice of the Peace, decided to intervene and met the Hosay procession outside San Fernando, asking them to return to their various estates. When they refused, Child himself ordered the police to shoot. Four demonstrators were killed and fifty others were seriously wounded. Brothers from St James and other Hosay centres boarded trains for the area and later that day, in Mon Repos, attacked the police with sticks and cutlasses. The battle left twelve more demonstrators dead and one hundred wounded.

These efforts of the rebellious groups were not chronicled by religion, but rather by ethnic origin and it is remarkable that in the Mon Repos skirmish, African Trinidadians were predominant, such was the brotherhood.

For the next sixteen years, the observances were contained on the sugar estates or abandoned altogether. It is against this multi-ethnic backdrop and historical perspective, that St James, perhaps the most cosmopolitan community in Trinidad and Tobago, continues the annual commemoration.

Opposite page
Hosay celebrations in Cedros, top, and St James

N. NORTON

J. BROWNE

N. NORTON

J. BROWNE

J. BROWNE

A Trinidadian family at Christmas

R. COOK

Children dressed as Christmas trees during the Christmas street parade in Port of Spain

S. BAHADUR

Previous page
Preparing for an Orisha festival

S. BAHADUR

Marching drummer boys during the Christmas street parade in Port of Spain

S. BAHADUR

S. BAHADUR

A lion dance and a traditional display to celebrate the 50th anniversary of the People's Republic of China

R. COOK

J. BROWNE

J. BROWNE

J. BROWNE

Above - Emancipation Day parade

Left - The festival of Santa Rosa. This cross-cultural celebration combines Christian and Amerindian beliefs and takes place in Arima, the only remaining location in Trinidad and Tobago that has an Amerindian population

Opposite page
Divali Nagar dancers in Chaguanas. Divali is the Hindu Festival of Lights which signifies the end to weeks of fasting and abstinence. The climax to this event involves the lighting of thousands of deeyas (small clay pots filled with oil) which are placed throughout homes and places of worship

N. NORTON

N. NORTON

Above - Children celebrating Phagwa. Also known as Holi, Phagwa heralds the arrival of Spring. Along with music and dance, this Hindu festival requires participants to throw abeer (pink-coloured water) at each other as a sign of good luck and fertility

Left - Decorated floats during the Indian Arrival Day celebrations

Opposite page
Moko Jumbies at the Heritage Festival in Tobago

Overleaf
Phagwa celebrations in Caroni

J. BROWNE

N. NORTON

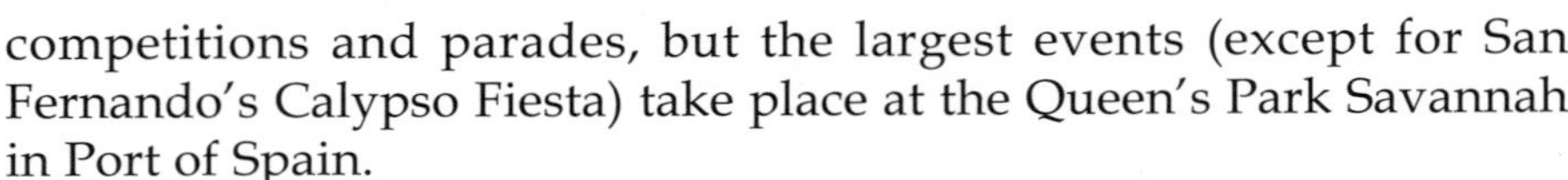

competitions and parades, but the largest events (except for San Fernando's Calypso Fiesta) take place at the Queen's Park Savannah in Port of Spain.

Each year new champions of calypso, soca, pan, extempo and mas are crowned. The best calypsonian and the most striking individual mas portrayals are normally determined on Carnival Sunday night, mere hours before the Mayor of the Capital City declares the street parades officially underway. Pan supremacy is judged on Carnival Saturday night, while the best of the soca singers is known after the final of that competition, which takes place on the Thursday before the parade.

For each of the major events, a junior version is also staged. In fact, Kiddies Carnival offers many more opportunities for competition, as a number of private contests precede the national parade, which takes place on Carnival Saturday. Champion junior pannists, masqueraders and calypsonians often develop into adult performers, ensuring continuity and holding out a promise of many more Carnivals to come.

On Carnival Tuesday night, a traditional last lap affords the weary participants a final chance to dance to the music, but at midnight, the drums are silenced, singers lay down their microphones and the horns are muted, as Lent begins and the planning cycle quietly begins once more.

S. BAHADUR

The origin of Carnival

There are those who insist that Trinidad Carnival is traceable to ancient Greek mythology, citing the rites of Bacchus, the God of Wine and other party components, as the major inspiration.

More popular is the view that as a feast of - and farewell to - the

S. BAHADUR

MINISTRY OF INFORMATION

flesh (Carne Vale), its origins are rooted in religion, since the final parade falls immediately before the Christian period of Lent.

But the influence of the French, who were invariably Roman Catholic, cannot be overlooked in favour of more romanticised versions. Many of the terms in Carnival are of such origin and the masked balls held by French gentry in the late 18th Century, which served as a precursor to today's style of revelry, seems to hold more weight than even the Greek god who, without expressed consent, lent his name to the bacchanalian festival.

The balls must have impressed onlookers, who were mainly slaves and who attempted to mimic their masters or parody them, giving rise to a number of Carnival portrayals that have survived even up to today. The Jab-Jab (from the French "diable"), the rambunctious Dame Lorraine and verbose Pierrot Grenade, are but three examples of that influence.

But there are also Spanish influences like the Burrokeet (or little "burro") and a number of suggestions that pander to none of the colonial dominions.

Stilt-walkers, called Moko Jumbies and the fearsome Midnight Robber are clear indications that from early in its history, Carnival was affected by other indigenous persuasions.

Slaves seeking to replicate the masked balls of the French were required to confine their mimicry to small pockets on estates until emancipation in 1838. From the following year, Carnival became an annual festival and, with the exception of 1941 to 1945 - when the festival was banned because of the Second World War - it has survived to today.

R. COOK

N. NORTON

although the people carrying them cannot be depended upon to hold still while the powerful music of live bands or disc jockeys blares at the northern end of the stage. A big band may have as many as six separate music systems, each delivering upwards of 20,000 watts of power.

By sunset, those bands that have completed the round of competition venues, now play for all who wish to 'jump-up', swelling the ranks to many thousands of revellers who will dance non-stop until midnight.

Monarchs of all they survey

Carnival royalty is selected from every facet of the festival. The King and Queen of Carnival are decided from entrants who represent mas bands at the level of leadership, although the bandleader seldom presents the portrayal on stage.

Elaborate costumes, some more than twenty feet high, are danced across the stage by the King and Queen of each band and judges sift the entrants to determine the best eight portrayals in each category.

TOBAGO FEST

Although Tobago shares the national festival, a second Carnival, exclusive to that island, was developed in 1998. Tobago Fest, takes place in October and is a collaboration between the Trinidadian band leaders and Tobagonians. The event is primarily a tourist-oriented activity, designed to boost the low season. However, it is beginning to attract large numbers of domestic as well as foreign tourists.
Terry Joseph

The finalists meet at Dimanche Gras on Carnival Sunday night, at the end of which that year's King and Queen of Carnival are announced.

A Junior King and Queen of Carnival are determined on the Carnival weekend through a separate contest, while the King and Queen of Jouvert are selected on the Monday morning of Carnival. The festival itself is frequently described as "The reign of the Merry Monarch."

R. COOK

The Road March

From the more than three hundred calypsos that are released during any Carnival of recent vintage, one emerges as the perfect trigger for masqueraders to lose all inhibition while performing in public.

That song is known as the Road March, an accolade that comes from the frequency with which it is played by disc-jockeys and bands on Carnival days. Normally, early indications come from the massive fetes, but there have been surprises.

Prior to 1993, the Road March was counted only at the Queen's Park Savannah venue on Carnival Days and the result available by the end of the festival. Today, it is now tallied at all official competition points in Trinidad and Tobago, which delays determination until all the scores are in from the various venues.

In the past, there was no real distinction between calypso and soca in this regard and there are many instances of the winning song in the national calypso monarch competition, doubling as the Road March. The last evidence of this to date came in 1986, when David Rudder won every competition available to him.

Since that time, there has been a clear distinction between these two entities and a new dimension introduced from the soca bands, who now produce their own songs, primarily for the purpose of copping this particular prize.

Although no poll is taken among the masqueraders, it is in the interest of the band leader to have his music systems play the song that he feels will give the greatest impetus to his members to jump-up and shake their bodies while parading before the judges.

Records are available since 1932, although official competition began in 1962.

In 1955, a European folk song, "The Happy Wanderer" was the most popular song on the road and in 1977 another foreign song, albeit a calypso, "Tourist Leggo", threatened to take the title, causing officials to declare that only home-grown calypsos are eligible.

The Carnival diaspora

Talented individuals who have emigrated to countries as far afield as Australia and South Africa, have developed Carnivals based on the Trinidad and Tobago model.

More than one hundred Trini-style Carnivals are on the calendar, although none of them has copied the dates of the Mother of All Festivals. Carnivals in foreign countries tend to fix the activity for a weekend preceding a public holiday, giving revellers the chance to recuperate after the jam.

Invariably, local artisans are hired to design, prepare and produce mas bands and assist with musical arrangements for steelbands participating in competitions in those countries.

The various components of Trinidad Carnival are reproduced to the extent that such activities are viable, with contests like the steelband panorama, soca and calypso monarch competitions, kings and queens of the mas bands and parades forming the basis of those productions.

An International Caribbean Carnivals Association has been formed to improve standards of the fledgling festivals.

West Indian communities in England and North America, where there are substantial numbers of Trinidadians, have established internationally recognised festivals like the Notting Hill Carnival in England, the Labour Day Carnival in Brooklyn, Montreal's Carifete, Carnival in Miami, and Caribana in Toronto.

Some countries have simply studied the format and attempted to implement it without reference to Trinidad and Tobago, but in most cases, expertise in the various areas of production of those festivals is sourced from this country.

Most recently, Ghana has joined the still growing list of Trini-style Carnivals, importing steelbands and mas producers to assist in getting the festival up and running.

S. BAHADUR

S. BAHADUR

S. BROADBRIDGE

R. COOK

S. BROADBRIDGE

S. BAHADUR

S. BAHADUR

S. BAHADUR

S. BAHADUR

S. BAHADUR

S. BAHADUR

MAS CHARACTERS

Dame Lorraine

A character from a mas satirising the French planters who introduced carnival to Trinidad. The Dame, in bonnet and long dress, is distinguished by her oversized bust and behind, both used to good effect when dancing

Moko Jumbie

The stilt dancer in brightly coloured trousers or full skirt is a descendant of the West African procession character, known for his ability to drive off malignant spirits or 'jumbies'

Midnight Robber

Identified by his huge-brimmed hat and cape, and his blood-curdling, bombastic speech. Originally inspired by cowboy costumes, the Robber has evolved so his hat may resemble a graveyard or even the Red House (Houses of Parliament)

Burrokeet

This donkey or horse mas has East Indian and South American origins. The 'rider' in his satin shirt and straw hat 'danced' his equally fine-costumed 'mount' to the accompaniment of strings and shac shacs

Pierrot Grenade

The scholar/jester proud of his ability to spell any word in his own fashion or to quote extensively from Shakespearean characters. Originally descended from the pierrot clown, noted for his elaborate satin gown decorated with sequins and bells and his white painted face

Jab Molassi

Dressed in shorts and wire tail, Jab Molassi (also known as 'Molasses Devil'), is smeared in grease, mud, and red, green or blue paint

Jab Jab

A 'pretty' devil in medieval jester's costume, covered in mirrors and rhinestones, with a plaited rope whip

Fancy Indians

One of the most spectacular mas characters at carnival. Originally based on the Native American Indian, the enormous and spectacular headpiece requires the support of a wire frame.

Bats

With wings that may span up to fifteen feet, and wearing claws on their hands and feet, this masked character is noted for its toe dancing, crawling, flapping and folding wings.

Simon Lee

S. BROADBRIDGE

Where music and social comment collide

Terry Joseph

WITH its lyrical content ranging from sublime to satirical, calypso is considered the musical mouthpiece of the masses, articulated by anyone brave enough to capture the essence of things and reproduce the information through witty rhymes and provocative commentary.

Cultural tradition has given the calypsonian extraordinary artistic licence, allowing the singer to touch on topics considered taboo by mere mortals. Early singers insisted that their lyrics were nothing but the truth, hence the term "lavway" (a corruption of the French "le vrai").

Indeed, many of the best-remembered songs of this century were based on actual events. The historic flight of the Graf Zeppelin; a security breach at Buckingham Palace; President Clinton's dalliance; the performance of local government; or mere gossip in the village rumshop; all provide the calypsonian with live ammunition.

Intimate details of actual or hypothetical relationships are not outside the realm of calypso, either, nor is total fiction, so long as the story allows the singer to articulate his particular philosophy on the subject.

Humour - a vital component in these compositions - often takes the form of "picong", an attack steeped in fact, but flavoured to suit the palate of inquisitive listeners. The fun is sometimes further cloaked in double-entendre, leading the uninformed to come away with one interpretation, while insiders revel in quite another.

MINISTRY OF INFORMATION

The Mighty Sparrow

The lyrics may be sung in standard English, assume the vernacular or move seamlessly between both styles. Choruses may either be repeated or supply fresh information at every opportunity. The rhythm of the music is guided only by the nature of the topic being addressed, but at Carnival time, the tempo would more than likely match the vibrant mood of the season.

Unlike other forms of music, the very nature of calypso, as a vehicle for public comment on the performance of high-profile individuals or groups, demands that new works be produced each year. And because of its link to the annual Carnival, these songs must be ready by January.

Much of the new work is presented via collectives called 'Calypso Tents' – a titular throwback to when the songs were performed in less sophisticated circumstances. Over the four weeks preceding the Carnival Parade, groups of singers appear nightly at the various tents.

A panel of judges visits each tent twice, selecting from among the hundreds of calypsonians interested in competing for the national title. The judges select the best twenty-four, each of whom is required to sing two pieces at a semi-final that whittles the group down to ten. On Carnival Sunday night, the ten finalists compete in a show called Dimache Gras.

From oil drum to musical marvel

Terry Joseph

WHILE the musical phenomenon of the tuned steel drum is more frequently described as the only acoustic instrument to have been invented in the twentieth century, 'pan', as it is affectionately known, can boast a whole lot more.

Not the least of its suppressed accolades is the fact that the very instrument is undoubtedly one of the more instructive examples of creative recycling. That discarded 55-gallon oil-drums could be retrieved from the dump-heap and re-fashioned into a symphony orchestra, supplies added-value to not just the drum, but also to the society in which the resulting music is performed.

There is an almost tangible native pride about pan. Visitors often experience true love at first hearing, although the sight of a steel orchestra in full flight also offers a unique brand of physical attraction. The full orchestra, which could involve as many as 150 players, utilises single drums for lead and solo work, playing along with double, treble and larger clusters, which are tuned to achieve the lower musical voices and effect precise chord-constructions.

More than one hundred steelbands are active in Trinidad and Tobago, although many are small ensembles, with consequently reduced ability to interpret complex orchestration. The big bands can, however, play all but sixteen of the piano's eighty-eight notes. In pieces where the written score exceeds the range of the band, the musical director often transposes the work to fit the pan scale, ensuring minimum interference with the composer's original intent.

In 1960, Pat Castagne (composer of the country's national anthem) wrote 'Treasure Island' as the test-piece for steel orchestras participating in that year's music festival, and Umilta McShine prepared 'Queen of the Caribbean' as the test for pan soloists. Since then, a growing cadre of indigenous composers have written primarily for execution by the steel orchestra. More recently, local composers are slowly turning the test of pan-virtuosity away from sheer dexterity at classical music.

At the annual Carnival, both large and small orchestras participate in a nationwide contest called 'Panorama', where each band is required to play at calypso tempo, either one of the popular dance-party songs of the season, or a piece specially composed for the occasion. A biennial steelband music festival is exclusive to the larger orchestras and includes adjudication of ensembles, quartets, trios, duets and soloists.

Pan music has travelled all over the world, several fine recordings are available and the instruments have been played at command

SOX
Potential Symphony
Potential Symphony
ENTIAL
MPHONY

performances for presidents and royalty. The global appreciation of pan continues to grow. No longer is it just a thing of mystique and novelty, but the sound of an orchestra with its own musical integrity.

Tuning the pan

Watching a skilled pan-tuner at work is a warm and fascinating experience. The ambient temperature is influenced not only by the heat of the flame he uses to help forge and temper the steel, but the pure excitement of being able to witness the detail of how a container designed to ship oil, or toxic chemicals is turned into a musical instrument.

Drums are selected and sanitised by the tuner, then the metal cover is removed from one end, while the other is hammered into a concave shape (a modern method uses spin-forming to create the concave).

After the sinking process, the notes are drawn from a template onto the playing surface and grooves are used to permanently define them. Some tuners drill holes along the groove to further isolate the notes.

The drum is then cut to the length that will be most faithful to the requirement of its tonal range. A tenor (or soprano) pan, which can host up to the thirty top notes in the band's musical spectrum, will be left with a skirt of about 15 cms. At the other end of the range, the bass pans, some with as few as three notes each, are left with full 76 cm of skirting.

The drums are now treated to the tempering process, using an open flame for heating. Part of the artisan's skill is that combination of knowledge and feel that allows him to decide on exactly when to remove the pans from the fire.

The tuner then uses hammers of various weights and sizes to tap the now isolated notes into submission, bringing each one individually to concert pitch and electronically testing accuracy at every sequence.

For both aesthetic and tonal reasons, the smaller pans in the orchestra are chrome-plated and swing from waist-high stands, whereas the bass-pans are normally painted and set on top of blocks of wood or suspended from racks that leave little space between their lower end and the ground.

The instruments are played with two sticks, the bass-player using a length and weight of mallet that uses sponge balls on the ends, while the soprano sticks use light materials, covered at one end with surgical rubber-tubing. Those pans that fall between the high and low end, use combinations of sticks and rubbers that offer the best reproduction.

When combined in orchestral formation and accompanied by rhythms (which include Latin-American percussion and wheel hubs beaten with pencil-thin poles of solid steel), the band can play any form of music from the latest calypso to the most intricate classical works.

Pan evolution

The first, unstructured noises came from garbage cans, which were played alongside the tamboo-bamboo rhythm sections that provided tempo for early Carnival parades and accompaniment for a form of indigenous martial arts called 'stick-fighting'.

Soon enough, the metallic sound ousted its host, replacing the dull thud of bamboo clatter altogether by presenting the player with identifiable notes and charting a different course for what would

eventually enjoy the status of government decree in 1992 as the official national musical instrument of Trinidad and Tobago.

But pan evolution also serves as a measurement of social change, its largest technical leaps running concurrently with broadening acceptance as a legitimate music. One of the more popular calypsos of the 1960s, The Mighty Sparrow's, 'Outcast', describes a scenario in which the pannist was ostracised simply on the basis of devotion to the instrument, which largely matched social positioning. Having been created by the descendants of slaves, the instrument has been forced to earn every rung of its acceptance.

The Africans that were brought over as slaves had to re-create from memory the musical instruments of their homelands. In addition, the artistic influences of their new environment had tampered with the authenticity of reconstructed articles.

By the late 1930s, coming more than one hundred years after the abolition of slavery, and as a result of the intervening influences, pan design had consequently forged its own direction. Although its most celebrated pioneers were those who had settled in the depressed Laventille and East Dry River areas where the cultural influences were predominantly African, the instrument no longer sought to duplicate that drum.

Like American blues and jazz, the creation of pan music was, therefore, more of an artistic expression triggered by the global economic depression existing at that time, rather than a distinctly African creation. And while World War II slowed pan development, by the turn of the fifties, the instrument's identity had already crossed the artificial boundaries of class, culture and ethnic origin.

MINISTRY OF INFORMATION

Names like Winston "Spree" Simon (who is widely credited with having played the first real melody on a tenor pan) and Elliott "Ellie" Mannette, who reversed the original convex shape of the instrument, no longer monopolised steelband conversation. Skilled players, tuners and leaders from other ethnic, social and cultural groups had already joined the fray.

By the turn of the 1950s, Alfonso Mosca and Zay Texiera, both of non-African heritage, were listed among the respected tuners and players. The four Figueroa brothers, sons of Venezuelan immigrants, were also regarded as good players. Roy Chin emerged as captain of Starland and the Dixieland Steel Orchestra, which was formed in 1950, comprising middle-class, college-educated boys, and three years later came a similarly comprised Silver Stars Steel Orchestras. This cross-fertilisation helped in no small way to spread acceptance of pan outward and upward, bursting free from its previous domain among the lower classes.

At the technical level, integration seemed complete when George "Whitey" Lynch was selected to join "Spree" on a 1955 teaching assignment to Nigeria. Seven years later, with the advent of the annual Panorama competition, the arrangers who took top honours for the first three years of that contest were of Indian descent. And at the national level, Jit Samaroo has not only led the inner-city based Amoco Renegades to an historic ten victories in the Panorama competition, but has led the country's most travelled steelband, The Samaroo Jets, for more than thirty of those years.

But in sociological terms, the steelband movement is a study in continuing evolution. Indeed, another dynamic is already evident, with women now comprising a growing percentage of the performing fraternity and junior competitions, coupled with images of success by internationally acclaimed virtuosos, encouraging youth into the fold. Mobility has also been boosted by the standardisation of many of the instruments and the switch to learning music, rather than internalising long and intricate passages by rote.

N. NORTON

F. KHAN

R. COOK

Above - Harris Promenade, San Fernando

Left - Butler Highway

Opposite page
Charlotte Street in Port of Spain

Page 88
Top - Store Bay, Tobago
Bottom - Matelot on the north coast

Page 89
Top - Pointe-a-Pierre
Bottom - Queen Street, Port of Spain

F. KHAN

Fishing port in San Fernando

R. COOK

B. ANTON

'Conch Man', Manzanilla

Crab-seller on the road to east Trinidad

Above left, down
River bathing at Grande Riviere

Water buffalo, or 'buffalypso', cooling down in Manzanilla

Ortinola Estate in the Maracas Valley

Opposite page
Top - San Fernando
Bottom - Yachts anchored in Scotland Bay, Chaguaramas

J. BROWNE

J. BROWNE

Manzanilla

Previous page
Top - Chacachacare Island
Bottom - Scotland Bay

F. KHAN

Above - Maracas Bay

B. ANTON

Mount Irvine Bay, Tobago

Opposite page
Top - Maracas Bay
Bottom - The mouth of the Mitan River in Manzanilla

F. KHAN

F. KHAN

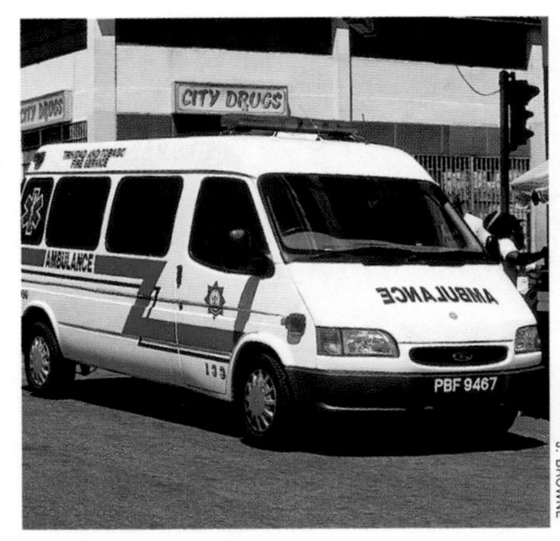

J. BROWNE

F. KHAN

F. KHAN

F. KHAN

J. BROWNE

Opposite page
Top - Trincity Mall near Piarco Airport
Bottom - Long Circular Mall, Port of Spain

F. KHAN

F. KHAN

F. KHAN

B. ANTON

F. KHAN

Main picture - Laventille
Above - Rock formation in Paria Bay
Above right - Crossing interchange under construction in San Fernando

F. KHAN

B. ANTON

F. KHAN

Main picture - Rafting on Grande Riviere
Above left - Old house on Chacachacare Island
Above - Coconut husker in Manzanilla

Williams Carenage in Chaguaramas

Page 108
Top - Looking east from Mount St Benedict
Bottom - Moka

Page 109
Top - The north coast of Trinidad
Bottom - Las Cuevas Bay

M. GASKIN

Above - *Estate workers returning home*

F. KHAN

Outdoor cooking in Blanchisseuse

F. KHAN

Opposite page
Maracas Bay

F. KHAN

Above - Maracas Bay

F. KHAN

Selling handicrafts at Gran Riviere on the north coast

Opposite page
Las Cuevas

M. GASKIN

J. BROWNE

Harvesting coconuts in Toco

J. BROWNE

Right - Burning sugar cane

Opposite page
Top - St Andrew's golf course in Moka
Bottom - A carpet of blossom petals surrounds a pink poui tree in Queen's Park Savannah

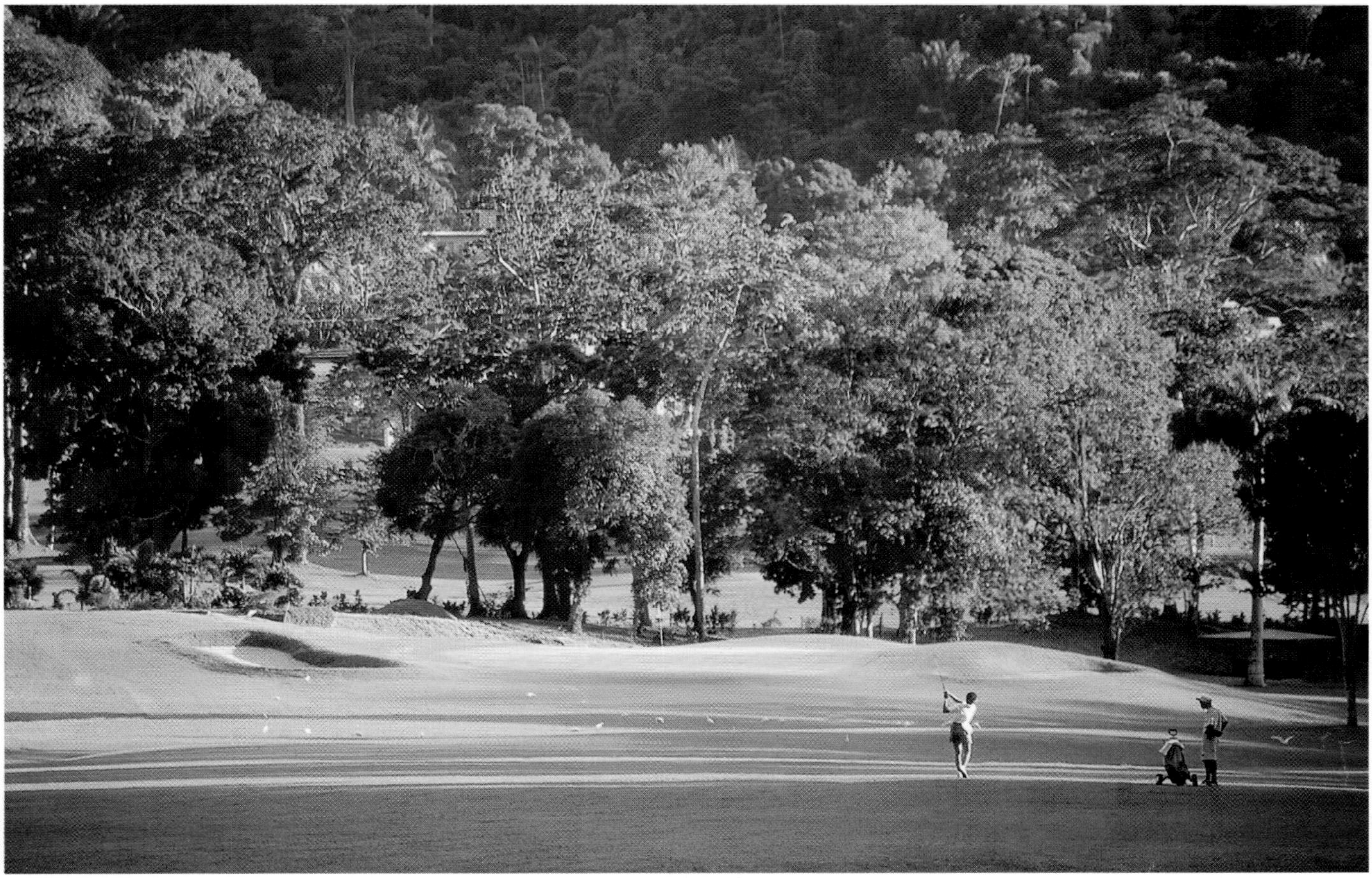

J. BROWNE

N. NORTON

R. COOK

N. NORTON

R. COOK

An old parlour at Erin Bay

R. COOK

Central market in Port of Spain

R. COOK

Central market in Port of Spain

YAMAHA

N. NORTON

Above - Bay near Charlotteville, Tobago

J. BROWNE

The headquarters of the Organisation of Eastern Caribbean States (OECS) situated in the Price Waterhouse building

S. BROADBRIDGE

Opposite page
Fishermen in Chaguaramas

J. BROWNE

Mayaro

F. KHAN

'Windball' cricket match in Trincity

J. BROWNE

Right - Rice laid out to dry

Opposite page
Pendulous nests of the crested oropendola hanging from the branches of an immortelle tree

M. GASKIN

Above - Toco lighthouse at Galera Point on the north-east coast of Trinidad. Tidal action from both the Atlantic Ocean and the Caribbean Sea, and the northern flow of the Orinoco River from Venezuela, make the seas around this coastline some of the roughest in the world

B. ANTON

Right - Balata Pool at the Maracas Waterfall in St George

Opposite page
Tompei River in Cumana on the north coast of Trinidad

N. NORTON

R. COOK

R. COOK

R. COOK

S. BROADBRIDGE

S. BAHADUR

F. KHAN

Almoorings Bay, Chaguaramas

The most exclusive island paradise

Simon Lee

Main building at Fort King George in Scarborough

TOBAGO is situated twenty-one miles off the north-east coast of Trinidad. This tranquil island is twenty-six miles long and stretches no more than nine miles at its widest point. It is unspoilt and ideal for relaxation and recuperation. With its crystal clear waters, spectacular coral reefs and white sand beaches, Tobago is one of the most exclusive destinations in the Caribbean.

Originally named Bells Forma by Columbus in 1498, Tobago was to become a pawn in the hands of various European colonists. Its 'ownership' changed nearly thirty times, between the Dutch, French and English, before being ceded to Britain in 1802. Tobago was made a Crown Colony in 1877, and unified with Trinidad in 1888.

But peace and tranquillity are what really characterises modern Tobago and its 50,000 inhabitants. Apart from the developed south-western tip - where most of the hotels are located - only the birds interrupt the serenity of the island. Even the capital, Scarborough, is little more than a small market town, nestling amid hills above Rockly Bay. Tobago's second major town is Plymouth, situated on the Leeward coast, with further settlements at Roxborough and Speyside on the Windward coast, and Charlotteville at the eastern tip.

For nature and eco-tourists, Tobago is a haven for more than two hundred bird species. Spectacular coral reefs add the finishing touches to a truly beautiful island paradise.

Right - Rock formation off the coast of Tobago known as the 'Three Sisters'

Opposite page
The Lagoon

'Bele Dancers' at Fort George

Offices of the Tobago House of Assembly

Right - Old church at Black Rock

Opposite page
Top - Scarborough
Bottom - View of Scarborough from Fort King George

J. BROWNE

B. ANTON

Charlotteville

Page 138
Top - Englishman's Bay
Bottom - Argyle waterfalls

Page 139
Charlotteville looking towards Giles Island

B. ANTON

B. ANTON

N. NORTON

R. COOK

Above - Goat racing

Right - Castara Bay

N. NORTON

J. BROWNE

Crab racing in Buccoo

N. NORTON

Above - *Speyside*

Left - *Government House*

N. NORTON

N. NORTON

Wedding ceremony in Moriah during the Heritage Festival

N. NORTON

Baking bread in an oven made from earth during the Heritage Festival

K. LEE

J. BROWNE

B. ANTON

Above right, down
North-west coast

President House

Main Ridge Reserve at the Bloody Bay Recreation Site

B. ANTON

J. BROWNE

K. LEE

Above - Tobago Museum at Fort King George

Left - Administration building, Tobago House of Assembly

B. ANTON

J. BROWNE

Right - St Francis Roman Catholic Church

Opposite page
Fisherman's hut at Parlatuvier Bay

N. NORTON

N. NORTON

B. ANTON

F. KHAN

N. NORTON

The Lagoon

B. ANTON

Page 146
Top - "Bambi" the fisherman is a well-known character in Tobago
Bottom - Back Bay

Page 147
Top - Pigeon Point
Bottom - Spectators await the start of 'The Great Race' at Store Bay

Page 150
Top - Cattle grazing at the Shirvah Estate
Bottom - Mount Irvine golf course

RAY 1664

N. NORTON

B. ANTON

K. LEE

A vibrant and dynamic capital city

S. BAHADUR

Frederick Street

F. KHAN

Brian Lara Promenade

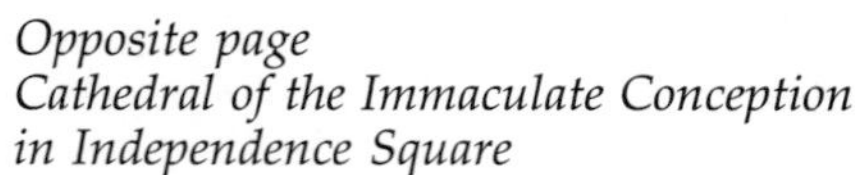

Opposite page
Cathedral of the Immaculate Conception in Independence Square

R. COOK

N. NORTON

S. BAHADUR

J. BROWNE

The Cenotaph in Memorial Park

S. BROADBRIDGE

Opposite page
Bottom - 'Monarch of the Sea', one of the world's largest passenger liners, docked at Port of Spain harbour

F. KHAN

F. KHAN

J. BROWNE

S. BAHADUR

Broadway seen from Independence Square

F. KHAN

J. BROWNE

F. KHAN

F. KHAN

'Pan Men' sculpture in Winston 'Spree' Simon Memorial Square

Unrivalled tourism with a difference

Simon Lee

TRINIDAD and Tobago is not usually considered as a typical Caribbean tourist destination, although you will find white sand beaches and tranquil turquoise waters. While little attempt has been made to develop the large scale tourism of islands like Barbados or Antigua, it is unrivalled in the Caribbean in terms of cultural, heritage and eco-tourism opportunities.

The country's unique cosmopolitan culture finds expression in Carnival which, with its music, dance and costuming, has won international recognition as "the greatest show on earth". But there are other equally unique festivals which outsiders are only now discovering - the Hindu festivals of Phagwa and Divali, the Muslim Hosay festival with its extraordinary tassa war drums, and Tobago's very own Heritage festival.

Trinidad's cultural range spans African retentions like the Shango and Orisha faiths, bongo and stickfighting songs and dances; and classical Indian song and dance. Traces of Spanish heritage are found in Christmas parang music and the French influence of the nineteenth century survives in the patois still spoken in the mountain village of Paramin.

Tobago has long been known as an exclusive, unspoilt hideaway with tourism development focused on small scale resorts. But the nation as a whole is as unique geologically as it is culturally, which makes it the most diverse ecological destination in the Eastern Caribbean. Once a part of mainland South America, much of the flora and fauna is reflected in the sub continent. With close to five hundred species of birds, including many of the most spectacular South American species, Trinidad and Tobago ranks high as an international birding destination.

Bio-diversity ranges from Tobago's coral reefs and the oldest protected rainforest in the western hemisphere, to Trinidad's mountains, rainforests, grasslands, mangroves, wetlands and mud volcanoes. Besides the birds, butterflies and bats, there are turtles nesting on the north coast and the endangered manatee in the Nariva swamp. Adventure tourists can kayak, snorkel or dive in Tobago, or mountain bike and hike in Trinidad.

Another rapidly expanding area of tourism is linked to the marina area of Trinidad's north western peninsula. Due to its position south of the hurricane belt, Trinidad is becoming increasingly popular as a yachting destination for pleasure, sport, repairs or simply for yacht-owners wishing to sit out the hurricane season in relative safety.

Page 160
Top - Maracas Bay

Page 161
Bottom - Beach facilities at Manzanilla on the east coast

PLEASURE GIRL

B. ANTON

F. KHAN

B. ANTON

F. KHAN

B. ANTON

F. KHAN

B. ANTON

K. LEE

Page 162
Top - Picnic at Salybia/Matura Falls in the Matura Forest Reserve, St David
Bottom - Moka Golf Course near Port of Spain

Page 163
Jetty at Pigeon Point, Tobago

Page 166
Top - Store Bay near Coco Reef
Bottom - Dive shop at Store Bay, Tobago

Page 167
Top - Almoorings Bay, Chaguaramas
Bottom - Yachts docked at Crews Inn

B. ANTON

B. ANTON

N. NORTON

N. NORTON

F. KHAN

B. ANTON

B. ANTON

Crews Inn Hotel

R. COOK

Casino in Maraval

F. KHAN

A BWIA passenger jet touches down at Piarco International Airport. BWIA is the national airline of Trinidad and Tobago and provides scheduled services throughout the Caribbean as well as regular flights to London and North America

Le Grand Courlan Resort and Spa at Black Rock, Tobago

Coco Reef, Tobago

Holiday Inn in downtown Port of Spain

F. KHAN

The Normandie hotel in Port of Spain

F. KHAN

Ambassador Hotel

N. NORTON

Trinidad Hilton

J. BROWNE

Kapok Hotel

F. KHAN

Blue Horizon Resort, Tobago

J. BROWNE

Chancellor Hotel, St Ann's

The splendour of an ecological carnival

Simon Lee

One of the balisier species of flower

IF you thought the Andes ended in South America, take a good look at Trinidad's Northern Range. These densely forested mountains rising to the main peaks of Cerro del Aripo (3,083 ft) and El Tucuche (3,072 ft) are a continuation of the Venezuelan cordillera and are the last link in the great Andean chain. If you need conclusive proof you can see it from the air flying south from Grenada or even on a clear day from Trinidad, when the mountains of the Paria peninsula are visible only seven miles (10 km) away across the Dragon's Mouth.

Trinidad and Tobago is unique not only for its cultural diversity but also for its bio-diversity. While historically, culturally, politically and economically it is part of the Caribbean, geologically and ecologically it belongs to the great South American sub-continent. Up to 15,000 years ago both islands were part of the mainland and recent evidence shows the existence of a land bridge connecting the south west tip of Trinidad to Venezuela less than two thousand years ago.

Consequently these two most southerly Caribbean islands share a range of flora and fauna which is not only unique but also unparalleled in the rest of the Caribbean. For the nature and eco tourist this twin-island nation is a paradise in miniature.

With a bio-diversity which includes coral reefs, coastal mangrove, salt and freshwater lakes, tropical rainforest, savannahs and grassland, mudflats and lowland forest all in the relatively small area of Trinidad's 1,864 sq miles (4,828 sq km) and Tobago's 116 sq miles, the country is home to nearly five hundred bird species, seven hundred butterflies, four hundred mammals, fifty-five reptiles and twenty-five amphibians.

If the statistics are impressive then the visuals are stunning: the scarlet ibis on its roosting flight over the Caroni Swamp; the iridescent dance of a ruby-topaz hummingbird only inches away; the sheer cliffs which drop 2,000 ft from the western approach to El Tucuche; the cascading cool waters of the Paria Falls or the slow underwater kinetic ballet of the myriad fish in the Nylon Pool - all these and more are ready to thrill with more colour and drama than carnival can offer.

The diversity that is the key to the country's ecology, begins with geology. In the north-east one moves from volcanic white quartzite to black basalt; on the east coast are smouldering sulphur rocks and there are more signs of volcanic activity down south in the world famous Pitch Lake; the mud volcanoes at the Devil's Woodyard, Lagoon Buffe in the Trinity Hills and Moruga Buffe, and the volcanic beaches at Erin and Icacos, where the red clay pebbles are streaked with yellow and blue.

Opposite page
Advocat waterfall

S. BROADBRIDGE

M. GASKIN

Above - The learning centre and breeding lake at the Pointe-a-Pierre Wild Fowl Trust

Opposite page
Golden poui tree in full bloom

There is even a sizeable coal mine in central Trinidad, and coal traces can be found on Chatham beach in the deep south. The south is, geologically, the youngest part of Trinidad, hence the volcanic activity and also the underlying oil-field.

Large limestone formations, at Paramin, Mount Tamana and Aripo, are relics of ancient coral reefs. The limestone is riddled with caves, a favourite habitat for the sixty species of bat. The members of a 'Discovery Channel' film crew on location at Mount Tamana, were convinced they had discovered the world's largest bat cave when they witnessed over a million bats on their evening exodus from a cave sunk deep in the flank of the hill.

For the dedicated adventurer there are endless hiking, biking, kayaking and diving options. Hikes range from easy walking to major expeditions. Many waterfalls can be reached with minimal exertion: five minutes from the Paria River bridge to the spectacular falls or a half-hour from the Windward Road in Tobago to the Argyll Falls. There are more demanding hikes like the ascent of Mount Tamana or the delightfully varied seven-mile trail from Charlotteville to Speyside, with a stop for snorkelling and a picnic lunch on Starwood beach.

In the strenuous but unforgettable category is the two to three day twenty-mile trek along the north coast from Blanchisseuse to Matelot where the only creatures you are likely to encounter are turtles, and which is the only Caribbean location where South American rainforest descends through montane forest to plunge directly into the sea. The assaults on the main Northern Range peaks of El Tucuche and Cerro del Aripo are full-day efforts.

B. ANTON

Yellow lily

The slow moving lowland rivers of Trinidad are ideal for kayaking

S. BROADBRIDGE

Above - View from the look-out tower at the Caroni swamp

Opposite page
Maracas waterfall

and wildlife observation. The Ortoire, which at twenty-five miles is the longest, flows east from the Central Range and with luck and some trepidation you might spot an anaconda or a cayman (a type of alligator). The white water North Oropouche rising in Aripo flows east through the Valencia Forest Reserve, which gives it an Amazon flavour.

Tobago is the scuba-diver's haven with sites for novices and the advanced. The Speyside, Charlotteville area is most popular for its excellent visibility and unspoilt coral including nearly all three hundred known South Atlantic species. The graceful and relatively friendly manta with its 10 ft wingspan is the most striking fish on the Speyside reef but you will encounter a vast ballet of angelfish, triggerfish, parrotfish, harmless barracuda and the smaller purple and gold fairy basslets, blackcaps, glassy sweepers, young yellowtails with their kinetic royal blue bodies stippled with electric blue spots, and the yellowhead jawfish.

On the Caribbean coast, the shallower sites with their minimal currents are favoured by underwater photographers who find perfect subjects in pink urchins, seahorses, spotted snake eels and gold-crowned sea goddesses. The wreck of the old ferry *MV Maverick*, a mile off Mount Irvine Point, is home to lobsters and thorny oysters, crabs and other crustaceans. The south coast sites which are vulnerable to tides and currents are for experienced divers, who might glimpse nurse sharks and sting rays relaxing in the sand where it meets the reef.

Among the larger fish encountered in Tobago waters are the blue marlin, white marlin and sailfish. Marine mammals like the sperm whale and bottle-nosed dolphin also frequent the waters around both islands.

Back on land there is an abundance of wildlife, which has long

J. BROWNE

Orchids

J. BROWNE

Above - The crested oropendola, locally known as the yellowtail or cornbird

Opposite page
"Fairy woods trail" at the Pointe-a-Pierre Wild Fowl Trust

attracted the attention of world experts. In the 1950s, pioneering naturalist and ornithologist William Beebe, the father of neo-tropical ecology, established a field research station for the New York Zoological Society at Simla in the Northern Range. Since then the former retreat of colonial governors has been home base for visiting naturalists and scientists.

In 1993, renowned British naturalist, David Attenborough came to film 'Vampires, Devil Birds and Spirits - The Calypso Isles', a study of Trinidad and Tobago's natural history, and he returned in 1998 to film the turkey vulture of Trinidad's Northern Range.

Wildlife species of global importance include the turtles, which nest along Trinidad's north and east coasts. Protected beaches at Matura and Grand Riviere are the sites for the world's largest density of nesting leatherbacks. In addition to these 6 ft long gentle giants, the shy hawksbill, olive Ridley and green turtle also nest here. There have even been reported sightings of the world's smallest and rarest marine turtle, the Kemps Ridley, which was thought to nest only on a beach in the Gulf of Mexico, moving up to the Mississippi delta to feed. Trinidad's proximity to the Orinoco delta, with its similar nutrients, may account for this discovery.

Another endangered species, the large, swamp-dwelling manatee, can still be found in the Nariva Swamp, one of the country's prime wildlife reserves. Nariva is the only freshwater swamp of any size in the southern Caribbean and provides sanctuary for migratory birds on their way from North to South America.

S. BROADBRIDGE

Iris

Given its South American origins, it is not surprising to find nearly fifty different snake species. Both the smallest and largest members of

M. GASKIN

Above - The lakes at the Pointe-a-Pierre Wild Fowl Trust are breeding grounds for many forms of wildlife including endangered species of birds, mammals and reptiles

Opposite page
Top - A unique location. The Pointe-a-Pierre Wild Fowl Trust is situated within a large petro-chemical complex
Bottom - Mangrove swamp at Manzanilla

J. BROWNE

the anaconda family are represented, the largest grows to 15 ft while its humble relative the worm snake is only inches long. Along with members of the harmless boa family - the macajuel, (constrictor), rainbow boa and cascabelle (tree boa) - there are four poisonous species, for which old hunters have their own secret remedy of antidotes. Besides two coral snakes there are two mapipires, the mapipire balsain (fer de lance) which grows to 8 ft, and the awesome mapipire zanana (bushmaster). Fortunately, the bushmaster, which grows up to 15 ft, prefers to remain undisturbed in the higher mountains.

Other reptiles include iguanas and tegu, the largest being the matte, which grows to 4 ft. As well as a profusion of crapauds (toads) and frogs whose nocturnal chorus fills the swamps, there is the endemic golden tree frog found on the highest mountains.

Another reminder of South America are the caymans. Familiar sights in the slow moving rivers and swamps, and occasionally seen crossing roads or highways, these 9 ft reptiles are less aggressive than their South American alligator cousins.

Trinidad's mammal family includes rare ocelots, tayra (a large weasel) and the peccary or quenk (wild hog), all residents of the mountains and rainforest. There are three species of manicou (opossum), agouti, tatoo (armadillo), two anteaters, a tree porcupine with prehensile tail, crab-eating racoons, deer, red howler and capuchin monkeys and the mongoose (introduced in 1870 to control the rats).

Among the species of bat, which account for sixty percent of the nation's fauna, are two different vampire bats, one which feeds off mammals and the other off birds. These bats may be the origin of the 'Soucouyant' folklore figure, the blood-sucking ball of fire. Other species

M. GASKIN

S. BROADBRIDGE

S. BROADBRIDGE

Above - The capuchin monkey is an endangered species

Opposite page
Teak trees

are content to feed on fruit and insects, although one is fond of fish.

In the air, the country is undoubtedly one of the world's, and definitely the Caribbean's, premier birding and butterfly destinations. The Amerindian name for Trinidad was "Iere" meaning 'Land of the Hummingbird', and today the island is home to sixteen different species of these exquisite, iridescent, jewel-like birds. With an estimated 460 bird species and seven hundred recorded butterfly species, Trinidad and Tobago has the world's highest density of birds per square mile and experts suggest it also has the highest density of butterflies. Tobago is home to 210 bird species, some of which are not found in Trinidad.

There are rare species like the oilbird, white-tail sabre wing hummingbird, tropic bird and blue-backed manakin; some of the most spectacular South American hummingbirds; rainforest species like honeycreepers and flycatchers, tanagers and toucans as well as migratory birds from North and South America.

The country has become increasingly popular with bird-watchers and ornithologists as a gentle introduction to the South American bird families. Although the subcontinent is home to 3,500 species, enthusiasts are forced to travel great distances over sometimes inhospitable or dangerous terrain. By contrast, Trinidad and Tobago, with its small scale, density of birds and easily accessible sites, offers all the excitement of South America but without the disadvantages.

Few natural dramas can compare with the roosting flight of Trinidad's national bird, the scarlet ibis, or the sight of the macaws flying through the sunset-silhouetted palms of Manzanilla.

The primeval rainforest of the Northern Range is luxuriant with a

S. BROADBRIDGE

Heliconia

F. KHAN

N. NORTON

Above - The Aripo Cottage is tailor-made for eco-tourists

Opposite page
Rincon waterfall

wide variety of trees - immortelles, silk cotton, balata, balsa, bamboo and bloodwood, cedar and cypre, mahogany and matchwood. Orchids, bromeliads and liana vines cling to the trunks of the upper tier, while ferns, heliconias and philodendrons cluster its undergrowth. Only a half-hour drive from Port of Spain brings you to the home of Papa Bois, folklore guardian of the forest and its creatures. Here, the greatest diversity of birds can be found.

The Pax Guest House, established in 1916 as part of Mount St Benedict, the Caribbean's oldest Benedictine settlement, nestles below the pine-tipped ridge of Mount Tabor, and has served as a nature lodge since the 1980s. This is the best location for viewing birds of prey, like the beautiful white and grey hawks, which nest on the abbey's estate, or the zone-tailed, short-tail and common black hawks, the turkey vulture and peregrine falcon, double-tooth and grey-headed kites.

The landscaped gardens attract an array of butterflies - cocoa mort bleu, scarce bamboo, flambeau and blue night. Flitting almost imperceptibly amid the undergrowth before it comes to a hovering halt by the flowers you might see a tiny tufted coquette, one of the world's smallest birds, its wings a blur of speed, or, with luck, the vibrantly decorated ruby-topaz hummingbird, unmistakable with its ruby crest blazingly distinct against its yellow breast.

The Asa Wright Nature Centre is not only Trinidad and Tobago's most famous eco-site, but one of the Caribbean's most important conservation areas and wildlife sanctuaries. Situated seven miles up the Arima Valley in lush rainforest, the 750-acre estate was established in 1967 on what had formerly been the Springhill cocoa and coffee estate. With its magnificent views over the forest canopy down the

S. BROADBRIDGE

Spider lily

B. ANTON

Egrets hitch a ride on the backs of cattle

Opposite page
Top - Nymphaea water lilies in the Nariva Swamp
Bottom - Hunter's lodge on the bank of the Ortoire River

valley vista all the way to the Montserrat Hills, the centre has become a major destination for international ornithologists, botanists, entomologists, naturalists, nature photographers and nature tourists.

Among the rare bird species to be seen are the nocturnal feeding oilbirds in the Diablotin Cave (the most accessible nesting site in Trinidad), the manakin lek and the white-neck Jacobin hummingbird. On the forest trails, expert guides will point out blue-crowned motmots, or rare white-bearded manakins displaying themselves in a copse of slender Bois L'agli, while overhead a bell bird tolls.

Without even stepping off the gleaming pitchpine floor of the old estate house veranda, visitors will see an endless procession of blue-chinned sapphires; emerald-chested hummingbirds; purple honeycreepers with their striking yellow legs; indigo cowbirds and silver-beaked tanagers. Over 170 of Trinidad's birds have been seen at Asa Wright.

Coming down from the rainforest there are many other excellent bird-watching locations. The Caroni Swamp, with its 12,000 acres of mangrove forests, tidal lagoons and marshlands, is a sanctuary for the ibis as well as the rare red-capped cardinal, and the stunning purple gallinule. The mangrove is also the habitat of the blue crab, an essential ingredient for the island dish of callaloo, while its brackish waters are thick with snook, salmon, grouper and mangrove snapper.

To spot Trinidad's rare endemic pawi (piping guam) might require scaling the heights of Aripo or heading for Toco on the north coast. The Arena Forest on the central mountain ridge is the haunt of spade-bills, woodpeckers and jacamars; the south-west peninsula is home to the yellow-headed parrots; and the southern Trinity Hills provide a habitat for black-hawk eagles.

J. BROWNE

Butterfly orchid

S. BROADBRIDGE

S. BROADBRIDGE

B. ANTON

Visitors watch the wildlife from the veranda at the Asa Wright Nature Centre in Arima

Opposite page
Blue-crowned motmot

West coast locations include the Waterloo mudflats, where the Sewdass Sadhu Hindu Temple keeps a watchful eye over the skimmers and waders from its vantage point in the sea, and the Pointe-a-Pierre Wildlife Trust. This sanctuary for endangered local wildfowl and migrant visitors, is unique even by Trinidad standards, situated as it is in the middle of an oil refinery compound.

In Tobago, the birds are as friendly as the islanders and there is little travelling involved in getting to see them. The national bird is the cocrico, but the most outstanding is the red-billed tropic bird, which nests on Little Tobago along with a rare species, the white-tail sabre wing hummingbird.

The Main Ridge Forest Reserve is the oldest protected forest in the Western Hemisphere. Established in 1776 by a colonial administrator, the reserve is home to the great black hawk, the rufous-breasted wren as well as flycatchers, woodcreepers and leaftossers.

In the wetlands of Buccoo Marsh, Bon Accord Lagoon and the Petit Trou Lagoon at Lowlands, rare species like the white-cheeked pintail, black-bellied duck and anhinga, are found alongside the family of waders from herons, grebes and plovers, to sandpipers and osprey.

Offshore islands serve as invaluable sanctuaries, while the pristine turquoise waters of the Caribbean Sea provide feeding grounds for pelicans, boobies, terns, petrels, jaegers, shearwaters and frigates.

If Trinidad and Tobago boasts of its carnival (and by extension its incredibly creative cosmopolitan culture) as "the greatest show on earth", it can also take pride in being blessed with the most unique flora and fauna, and the most diverse ecology of the southern Caribbean.

N. NORTON

Cocoa pods

N. NORTON

F. KHAN

Above - Pink poui tree in bloom in Queen's Park Savannah

Right - Angel Valley waterfall

S. BROADBRIDGE

Opposite page
Lalaja Falls on the Marianne River in St George

Overleaf
The West Indian manatee - found in eastern coastal waters, inland ponds and rivers and in the mouth of the Nariva Swamp. The manatee is an endangered species

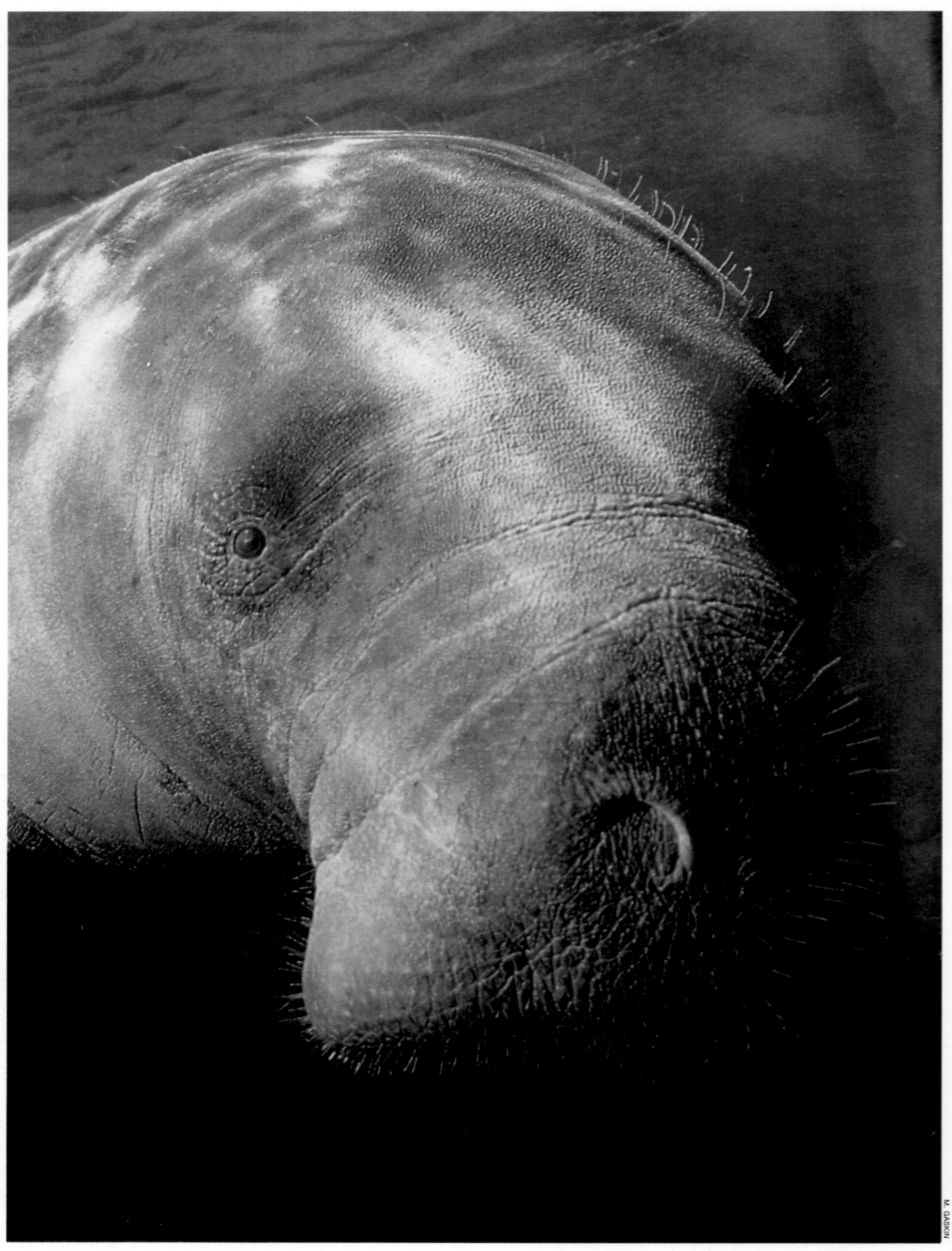

M. GASKIN

N. NORTON

F. KHAN

B. ANTON

Dolphins off the coast of Huevos

Coral reefs around Trinidad and Tobago provide a spectacular array of marine life

Previous page
Top - Scarlet ibis in flight
Bottom - Buffalo, locally known as 'Buffalypso', on the beach at Manzanilla

S. BROADBRIDGE

Ginger flower

B. ANTON

Green honeycreeper

B. ANTON

Chestnut woodpecker

Historic and sublime places of interest

F. KHAN

The lighthouse in Toco

J. BROWNE

Gaspree Caves

B. ANTON

Fort George in St James

F. KHAN

F. KHAN

J. BROWNE

From top right, down
Red House, the Houses of Parliament, Port of Spain

The National Museum

Sangre Grande Police Station

F. KHAN

J. BROWNE

Monument commemorating Indian arrival situated in Cedros

F. KHAN

J. BROWNE

From top left, down
Whitehall, the office of the Prime Minister

Queen's Royal College

Public Library at the Hall of Justice, Port of Spain

J. BROWNE

Chaguaramas Hotel & Convention Centre

F. KHAN

Military museum in Chaguaramas

F. KHAN

F. KHAN

B. ANTON

From top right, down
Crews Inn, Chaguaramas

The Ministry of Foreign Affairs

Mount St Benedict in St Augustine

R. COOK

J. BROWNE

The beach at Grand Chemin, where Christopher Columbus first set foot

F. KHAN

From top left, down
The Pitch Lake in La Brea

Stollmeyer's estate house in Santa Cruz

Police Training College, St James

J. BROWNE

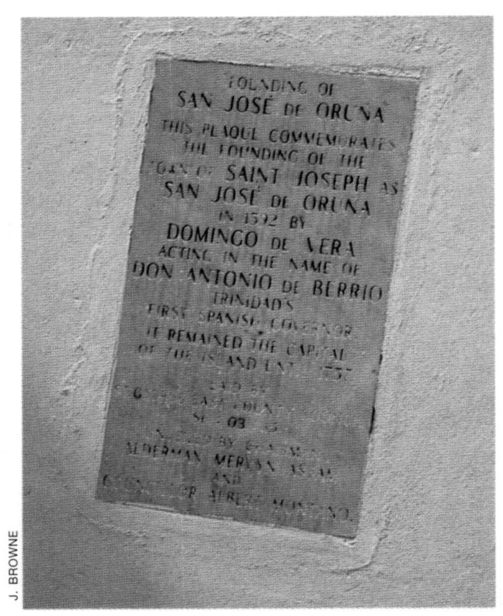

J. BROWNE

Plaque in St Joseph commemorating the site of Trinidad's first capital

K. LEE

Above - The largest silk cotton tree in Tobago. The tree was considered sacred by African slaves

Right - Large wooden plaque citing 150-year-old history of sacred silk cotton tree

K. LEE

From left, down
The Sewdass Sadhu Mandir in Waterloo is known as the 'temple on the sea'

The Lopinot Complex in Arouca was once a cocoa estate

Spring Bridge in Blanchisseuse

F. KHAN

B. ANTON

B. ANTON

K. LEE

The inscription on the Stiven family tomb in Tobago remains an unsolved mystery

S. BAHADUR

Ceremony to mark the opening of the Hall of Justice

N. NORTON

Right - Lion House in Chaguanas

N. NORTON

Stollmeyer's Castle

J. BROWNE

Toco Folk Museum

N. NORTON

The Town Hall in San Fernando

J. BROWNE

Ambard House

S. BAHADUR

President's House

S. BROADBRIDGE

Fort San Andreas behind the old sea wall in Port of Spain. In the background is the old railroad building

B. ANTON

Nun's quarters on Chacachacare Island

The architecture of individualism

Simon Lee

THE English writer Patrick Leigh Fermor, when catching his first glimpse of the Magnificent Seven, those exuberantly iconoclastic mansions which adorn the western side of the Queen's Park Savannah in Port of Spain, went into paroxysms of delight over "these gorgeous follies... with their crazy, defiant architecture."

J. BROWNE

Trinidadian architecture is as individualistic, eclectic and diverse as the callaloo of cultures which have made their homes here. In addition to the Amerindian, European, African, Asian and American influences, there is also a definite Trinidad Creole-style, evolved from the same spirit of creativity and experimentation that animates Carnival.

While the traditional architecture of Tobago is more restrained, the characteristic 'Trini' individualism is immediately apparent from even a cursory glance at any of the modern housing developments on and off the east-west corridor. The basic unit is invariably added to or embellished, reflecting the owner's taste and desire to be different from their neighbours.

In the aftermath of independence and the heady days of the oil boom, much of the architectural heritage was abandoned or destroyed in the thrust toward constructing a modern Trinidad and Tobago. This was the era when the Twin Towers and the Eric Williams medical complex - monuments to self determination - were built.

Fortunately, in the 1990s, a new spirit of preserving the cultural heritage has emerged, so that although unique buildings like Bagshot House in Maraval have disappeared, Whitehall, one of the Magnificent Seven, has been restored and now serves as the Prime Minister's office.

J. BROWNE

An afternoon's drive from Port of Spain across the Caroni plain to the Montserrat Hills, takes you from the old barracks, gingerbread houses, colonial mansions and air-conditioned office blocks and shopping malls of town, past cathedrals, mosques and mandirs, through East Indian villages where you can still find mud houses (traditionally plastered with cow dung) and on to the old cocoa estates where some of the great houses survive. In Tobago there are still a few of the plantation great houses, like Richmond Great House, from the days when sugar was 'king'.

Before any Europeans arrived, the Amerindians built ajoupas, simple wattle and daub, palm thatched huts, which were ideally suited to the climate. Either open sided or with low walls of woven branches or reeds filled with mud, the ajoupas were cool and waterproof and easy to dismantle or simply abandon before moving on. Examples of this early style are the replica Amerindian huts in Cleaver Woods just

Stollmeyer's estate house in Santa Cruz

Old houses in Laventille

outside Arima and the beautiful ajoupa, with its tall peaked thatched roof, in the grounds of the Kariwak Hotel in Tobago.

In 1592, the Spanish established Trinidad's first capital at San Jose de Oruna, in the foothills of the Northern Range, above the mosquito infested mangrove swamps. Once they had laid out the town square with its cabildo and church they soon abandoned any pretence at imperial architecture. A report to the Spanish King in 1612 mentions "thirty-two straw huts" and a letter of 1637 describes houses "made of earth stamped solid which they call tapias and roofed with thatch."

Even as late as 1777, the relocated capital Port of Spain was, in reality, no more than a fishing village consisting of "houses made of mud and grass and thatched with palm leaves."

It was the influx of French settlers who made the first major contribution to architecture since the Amerindians. From 1783, fleeing the French Revolutionary tremors in Haiti, Guadeloupe, Martinique, St Lucia and Grenada, the French planters poured in. With them they brought a Creole style which they had evolved in the other islands, to suit tropical conditions: wide covered galleries for shade; jalousie

Boisierre House , Queen's Park Savannah

F. KHAN

S. BROADBRIDGE

Morgan's House, 'Roomor', Port of Spain

N. NORTON

R. COOK

From top left, down
High-rise apartments in Port of Spain

The Town Hall and bandstand in San Fernando

'The Greens', a development of condominiums in Maraval

From modern art to the sounds of the past

Raymond Ramcharitar

John Young's 'Hands of Magic' craft shop in Manzanilla

WHILE the 1.3 million living people in Trinidad and Tobago could be contained in any small metropolitan city, the sheer variety in their social and ethnic customs, and their creativity, would occupy several countries.

The desire to have a good time is legendary. This much is visible following their migratory routes to North America and Britain. Every place they have settled - from San Francisco to Boston, New York to London - has seen the emergence of a version of the Trinidad-style Carnival.

The world famous Trinidad Carnival, encompasses every genre of artistic activity fusing sparks of African, Indian and European culture into a single flame. From Christmas to the start of Lent, the country is absorbed in the fervour of preparation in time for the fever of Carnival.

The rest of the year sees the arts fragmented into their separate orbits. Out of the Carnival nexus, though, comes a heavy orientation toward music. Rapso and chutney, two new musical styles formed here in the last twenty years, occupy much of the entertainment calendar. Rapso is a mix of spoken poetry and sung lyrics. Chutney is sung in Hindi to rapid percussive rhythms using raunchy lyrics.

Concerts showcasing them vary in size from a cafe or bar, to a packed stadium, with invited Jamaican DJs like Sizzla, Ninja Man and Beenie Man, among others, to perform alongside. A few American pop acts, like Roberta Flack and Lauryn Hill are thrown in for good measure. Separately, Indian film stars and singers also perform here to sold-out audiences.

In recent years, the potential of culture as a revenue-earner, has given rise to a deliberate cultivation of musical events. October has been dubbed 'entertainment month', and among the events planned is a World Beat Music Festival, which invites musicians like Baba Maal, Ravi Shankar and Hugh Masakela.

The events are fixed in their months, but it is impossible to tie down the concerts to a particular time of the year, though there is some concentration around the public holidays, Easter and summer. Complementing these big events are smaller cabaret shows and stand-up comedy performances which abound in the cities' bars and cafes.

For movie buffs, there are fifty or so cinemas spread throughout the nation showing up-to-date British and American films and Bollywood movies - India's answer to Hollywood.

Opposite page
Top - Artist, Winston I Steward at work
Bottom - Carib Parranderos, Arima

J. BROWNE

N. NORTON

PARANG - A TRADITIONAL SOUND AT CHRISTMAS

When the Christmas season draws near, the music Trinidadians expect to celebrate with while they feast on ham, black fruit cake, sorrel drink and rum is 'parang', a vibrant reminder of the nation's Spanish heritage.

The main aspect of traditional parang is celebrating the story of the Nativity in songs to the accompaniment of strings and percussion instruments. These 'aguinaldos' and 'serenales' sung in a distinctly Trinidadian version of Spanish, were introduced during the nineteenth century by Venezuelan peons who came to work on cocoa estates and settled in the valleys of the Northern Range.

But the word 'parang' comes from a more secular activity and series of songs which the peons also brought with them. 'Parrandear' in Venezuelan means moving from place to place with no time limit, enjoying oneself. From October, groups of parranderos would roam from one mountain village to the next, stopping to play the sacred aguinaldos but also lively joropos, manzanares and guarapos in exchange for rum and a little food.

Traditional parang still survives and in season parang groups like The Lara Brothers and the San Jose Serenaders, dressed in Latin style, can be heard playing throughout the islands.

The main instrument is the cuatro, a miniature four-stringed guitar, which provides a distinctive percussive rhythm. It is backed-up by Spanish guitar, the mandolin and bandolin which provide tenor melodies. Violin and cello are optional but chac chac (maracas) is essential percussion for the parang sound, supported by scraper and hand drum.

In recent years hybrid forms like parang soca and parang chutney soca have developed. These are generally sung in English with risqué and humorous lyrics more often associated with calypso. *Simon Lee*

J. BROWNE

J. BROWNE

Above right, down
Renowned parranderos, the Lara Brothers

Kenny J, well-known calypsonian

The local landscape has traditionally provided a vast granary of stories - drama, romance, melodrama and action - and sometimes these are brought to life by locally-produced television drama serials.

The arts are represented by many talented individuals both in literature and fine art, and there is a high standard of theatre, classical music and performing arts.

St Lucian-born Nobel Laureate, Derek Walcott established the Trinidad Theatre Workshop in 1959 and it has become the vanguard of theatre in Trinidad and the Caribbean. The organisation focuses on Walcott's own theatre productions, and quality Caribbean drama using performers and directors from throughout the region. A small commercial theatre circuit exists through a few active companies who concentrate on the production of American and British farces and light comedies.

Dance is represented by a handful of studios, the most established being the Astor Johnson Repertory Company in Port of Spain, and the visual arts scene comprises around two hundred artists who maintain year-round exhibitions in the capital.

N. NORTON

Limbo dancing

J. BROWNE

Ken Crichlow, artist at work

S. BAHADUR

Spectacular artwork at Central Bank produced by artist and author Willi Chen

A wealth of literary talent and diversity

Kris Rampersad

TRINIDAD and Tobago's literary accomplishments defy its size. The sons and daughters of its two islands have claimed almost all the existing accolades for literature offered by the international community.

The various cultures, beliefs and languages that feed into the society, present writers with a kaleidoscope of experiences from which the rich mosaic of the nation's literature has evolved. The New World society, which, until the early 20th Century possessed no literary tradition of its own, facilitated an open-mindedness to writing styles from traditions in other parts of the world. The society benefited from exposure to the rich tradition of Western literature that sprang out from Grecian civilisation and passed into British literature; the ancient literatures of the East by descendants of immigrants from India, China and Syria; and an oral tradition through which the culture of India and Africa were initially transmitted to first and second generation Trinidadians.

But it was some time before writers were confident enough to use images and metaphors, and to write about local subjects, settings and situations, and in styles and a language of their own. The indigenous creativity that was reflected in primary forms of expositions (oral renditions like calypso) did not find expression in literature until the 1930s.

The birth of literature was engendered by the emergence of the society from slavery, indentureship and colonialism into self-assertion, self-expression, self-identification and independence. Most of the early writers of fiction started as journalists, clamouring for social and political reform. Then, in the 1930s, two magazines were launched in Trinidad that set the pace for continued literary exploration - *Trinidad*, and *The Beacon*. Among the contributors were the founders of West Indian literature - CLR James, Alfred Mendes, Ralph De Boissiere and Albert Gomes. James went on to become recognised as a poet, philosopher, short story writer and historian, whose works, *Beyond a Boundary* and *Black Jacobins* are considered the Bibles of cricket, and the Haitian Revolution, respectively. Meanwhile, the Indo-Trinidad press was nurturing such writers as Seepersad Naipaul, H.P. Singh and Dennis Mahabir. Naipaul, who also worked as a journalist with the *Trinidad Guardian* and published a collection of short stories in 1953, *Gurudeva and Other Indian Tales*, was the father of V.S. Naipaul - acclaimed as one of the best writers of the English language - and Shiva Naipaul, and grandfather of Neil Bissoondath, whose stories and articles have set the pace for discussions on multi-culturalism in Canada.

The grounding in journalism set the stage for the outpouring of novels of social realism and satire that characterised the 1950s and

1960s. Trinidadian writers like V.S. Naipaul, Samuel Selvon, Sonny Ladoo and Ismith Khan, and St Lucian-born Derek Walcott, migrated to the metropolises of the world in search of intellectual stimuli and a reading audience. Their themes were those that were occupying the debates at home and the international arena - themes of migration, dislocation and displacement; the sense of futility and anomie when up against the larger world. Walcott's attempts to carve epic space through his poetry eventually won him the Nobel Prize for Literature in 1992 with his publication of *Omeros*. Walcott began his literary career as a poet and playwright in Trinidad and founded the still vibrant Trinidad Theatre Workshop. His flexibility with the language, and manner of collating the collective experience of not only the region, but the world, has influenced successive generations of West Indian poets. His poetry has inspired several generations of poets and writers, including Ramabai Espinet, a Trinidadian woman writing out of Canada. Naipaul, several-time nominee for the Nobel Prize, holds most other literary awards, including the Booker Prize, Britain's highest literary award.

At a time when writers were suffering from pangs of conscience that they were stiffly copying English, Selvon successfully created a dialect voice that he used not only in dialogue, but also in narrated prose. It earned him credit for giving literary credence to the West Indian voice. It is utilised in his novel, *The Lonely Londoners*, a classic on the experiences of West Indian migrants to the United Kingdom.

Among those who stayed at home, and continued writing prolifically is Michael Anthony, historian, short story writer and novelist. His novels are gentle expositions on childhood and adolescence in Trinidad. On the other hand, Earl Lovelace, holder of a Commonwealth Writer's Prize, who also pursued his writing career from Trinidad, writes mainly about adulthood, as a metaphor for a society in the process of maturation.

Several new voices have been emerging. Trinidadians, writing from diasporic satellites in Canada, North America and Europe, continue to enrich the mosaic. Lawrence Scott is a published novelist and short story writer, writing out of the European-Trinidadian experience; Willi Chen is a painter who has taken his sensitivity to colour and detail into short story writing; and Claire Harris, writing from Canada, echoes the struggles of minority communities. The latter half of the century has also seen the emergence of Wayne Brown, poet; Faustin Charles, novelist writing out of England; Tobago-born Eric Roach, whose poetry has been aired on BBC's Caribbean Voices programme; poet Victor David Questel; painter and poet, Leroy Clarke; Clyde Hosein; Ken Parmasad, Sharlow Mohammed, Lakshmi Persaud, Jennifer Rahim, Cynthia James-Rudder, Christopher Laird, Isaiah James Boodhoo, and Vishnu Ramsamooj. Among the exponents of "voice" literature are Paul Keens-Douglas whose vernacular poems overflow with anecdotes and local humour. His brand of literature captures the vibrant resonances of the spoken word, and the satire, humour and social conscience of calypsonians like Sparrow, Kitchener, The Roaring Lion, Chalkdust, Calypso Rose, and The Gypsy.

Literary development in Trinidad has been enhanced by development of a living critical tradition. A new wave of writing is now exploring children's stories and biographies, and it is hoped that the home-grown mystery and thriller novel will, soon, join the long list of literary achievements.

A culinary blend of traditional flavours

Annabelle Ove

J. BROWNE

Charlie's restaurant in St James

F. KHAN

Columbo Restaurant in San Fernando

"YOU are what you eat", claims the old adage, and nowhere is this more poignant than in Trinidad and Tobago, where a rich blend of cultures and traditions has given rise to the most unique culinary delights.

The Europeans may have come in search of 'El Dorado', but when their quest proved fruitless, they embarked upon another course and developed a little treasure for themselves.

In the bitter sweet days of slavery, when sugar was the main course, colonists imported an abundance of fruit and vegetables, including mangoes, citrus fruit, bananas, rice and breadfruit. Today, a leisurely stroll through any of the many markets provides testament to the agricultural prowess of those early immigrants.

All the necessary ingredients for most of the island's traditional dishes are available in great numbers - bright green dasheen leaves, okra and blue crabs for callaloo (a variation of gumbo); deep purple melongene (aubergine) and vivid red tomatoes; large yams, sweet potatoes and eddoes, all root vegetables known locally as "blue food".

Fruit, too, is grown and enjoyed in equal measures - pawpaw (papaya), pineapples, pomerac (similar to an apple), guava, soursop, sapodilla, mangoes, and the many varieties of banana.

The islands are also blessed with a constant supply of fish from seas nourished by the delta waters of the Orinoco River flowing from South America. Grouper, king fish, red snapper and shrimp are some

F. KHAN

BLACK CAKE
Rich, iced and decorated cake made with dried fruit soaked in cherry brandy and rum, baked and re-soaked. A traditional wedding cake

BULJOL
Shredded saltfish with onions and tomatoes, avocado, pepper and olive oil

CALLALOO
Savoury soup, made with okra, dasheen leaves and seasonings, often flavoured with hot pepper and whole blue-backed crab

DOUBLES
Curried channa (chick peas) between two bara (soft, fried dough), sold by road-side vendors

HOPS
Crisp bread roll, filled, for example, with ham (ham 'n' hops)

PASTELLES
Patties of minced meat seasoned with olives and capers, folded in pure corn dough, wrapped in banana leaves and steamed. A Christmas speciality

PELAU
Peas and rice, cooked with meat and flavoured with coconut and pepper

PHULOURI
Fried fritters made with split peas

ROTI
Curry wrapped in a cooked, pancake-like dough (may be filled with split peas, 'dhalpuri')

SOUSE
Pork, boiled and served cold in a salty sauce with lime and cucumber, and pepper and onion slices

J. BROWNE

F. KHAN

J. BROWNE

From top, down
Coconut vendor in Manzanilla

'Angie's' situated in La Brea, specialises in lime pepper sauces and pickles and is popular with many Trinidadians

Loy Peters' 'First and Last Bar' in Manzanilla

F. KHAN

Above - Thai Palace restaurant

F. KHAN

Right - Pizza Hut and KFC in La Romaine

of the many varieties available, as is shark, which provides the main ingredient for the popular 'shark 'n' bake'. Even mangrove swamps provide a banquet of oysters available from many road-side vendors and served in the shell or in a spicy cocktail sauce. Queen's Park Savannah provides another location for even more vendors offering a constant supply of roast or boiled corn-on-the-cob, and phulouri balls, all to be washed down with fresh coconut water or an ice cold sno-cone.

The East Indian community has influenced many of the island's most popular dishes. These include curry and rice or the nation's very own fast-food; 'roti', which is curry wrapped in a pancake-like dough; 'doubles', two small baras (soft fried buns) filled with channa (chick peas) and chutney, a staple breakfast meal; and 'buljol', saltfish with onions and peppers served with avocado.

J. BROWNE

The New Shay Shay Ten Chinese restaurant in Port of Spain

Creole food - a blend of African and Spanish or French influences - provides the basis of most home cooking and is also available in local restaurants and cafes. Popular dishes include brown stew chicken or beef, rice and peas accompanied by fried plantain, callaloo and coocoo (derived from the West African foofoo and made from boiled cornmeal), fried or steamed fish, and pork or chicken pelau. And no meal in Trinidad and Tobago would be complete without hot pepper sauce. Tobago reflects the same culinary tastes as her 'big sister', but there are some dishes which are unique including the not-to-be-missed crab and dumplings.

The sugar industry throughout the Caribbean gave rise to the production of rum, perhaps the most ubiquitous beverage in the region. Each island has its own varieties, and Trinidad and Tobago are no exception. The most notable distilleries, producing varying degrees of vintage and quality, are Caroni, Fernandes and Angostura. Angostura also produces the world famous Angostura Bitters, a product synonymous with Trinidad and Tobago, which is used in both drinks and food recipes.

Local beers and lagers, such as Carib and Stag, play an important role in the country's culinary tastes as do most of the international brews. However, a uniquely Caribbean drink like mauby is enough to quench any thirst, and a traditional drink of sorrel is the perfect seasonal touch to a truly Caribbean Christmas.

Opposite page
Top - Jenny's Wok restaurant in Port of Spain

Bottom - 'The Roxy' Pizza Hut

F. KHAN

J. BROWNE

Education is the key to sustainable growth

Lucretia Gabriel

TRINIDAD and Tobago has a long history of high attainment in education and, furthermore, the country was led into independence by two university professors - Dr Eric Williams and Dr Rudranath Capildeo.

The majority of children up to the age of four will spend much of their time in nursery schools. It is a system that developed naturally from more leisured times, when few women worked outside the home. With the easy availability of household help, and the Trinidadian extended family, children are generally well cared for, and parents experience few significant breaks in their employment.

Nursery schools developed as the number of working women increased as well as the appreciation of early childhood care. In addition, there are a significant number of Montessori nursery schools, where the emphasis is on learning through a child's own discovery.

The main aim of the nursery schools in general is to ensure that all children are able to take any entrance test to a 'prestige' primary school.

There are more than 94 primary schools that accommodate over 176,000 children. These schools are responsible for taking the pupils to their first milestone - the Common Entrance examination. At eleven or twelve years-old, this test marks an end to primary education. Success enables children to enter a college or secondary school of their choice. Outstanding results may also be rewarded with a scholarship or other similar incentives which are sponsored by the Government or private businesses.

The Government has introduced a Continuous Assessment Programme (CAP) into the primary education system. This will replace the Common Entrance exam which is to be phased out by 2004. Under this system, children would no longer advance to a higher class because of age, but rather by performance. This will benefit those children who have special learning needs and require a little more help before moving on.

The range and quality of primary schools is wide, and includes government as well as private institutions.

There are 478 secondary schools in Trinidad and Tobago with an additional fifty already planned. Secondary education is firmly based on the British system, and a complete range of subjects is taught, from the strictly academic to the vocational.

The secondary school system has two major examinations - the Caribbean Examination Council (CXC), for students aged fifteen plus, and Advanced or 'A' Level, for students aged seventeen plus. The

Opposite page
Top - Pupils of St Francis Primary School, Sangre Grande

Bottom - Warrenville Presbyterian School

J. BROWNE

F. KHAN

MEETING THE NEEDS OF THE NEXT CENTURY

The Government and the University of the West Indies (UWI) - with its local faculties - are constantly increasing the numbers and standards of the nation's Distance Learning Centres - created to accommodate studies in this fast-paced world of technology.

With the increasing demand for institutions which provide teaching in areas such as law and business management, the UWI, the Caribbean Union College and other tertiary institutions, along with the Government, are preparing for major educational change.

The Eric Williams Medical Sciences Complex and the National Institution for Higher Learning offer teaching for diverse careers in sciences. The UWI School of Business Management, School of Computer Science and Business, offer career training for the business environment. Technical courses are equally important and are available at established institutes such as the John Donaldson Institution, the San Fernando Technical Institutions and the Youth Training and Employment Partnership Programme. Graduate students from any of these institutions are considered to be some of the best in the Caribbean. Distance Learning Centres are becoming more widely available throughout the country as the Government and the Ministry of Education, along with the University of the West Indies and other educational institutions, address the challenges and developments of the 21st Century. *Michelle Lewis*

J. BROWNE

Above
Children from the Mucurapo Girls' school

Opposite page
Top - Muslim boys' school in Warrenville

Bottom - Administration Building at the University of the West Indies. The university was established in Trinidad in 1947 and this site is one of three autonomous campuses located in the Caribbean. The other two are in Barbados and Jamaica

CXC exam (taken from May to June) replaced the English Examinations Board's 'O' Levels. English and Maths are compulsory subjects, and most schools insist that students take a second language. In most cases this is Spanish.

The Government guarantees students an education up to the CXC examinations stage after which, approximately forty percent of students continue their education at 'A' Level.

Science and business subjects dominate this next stage of education, although recent emphasis on the environment has heightened the profile of geography, for which a national scholarship is now available.

Many students from Trinidad and Tobago continue their education overseas, usually in North America, the UK and Europe. In addition, there is the International School and the Maple Leaf School, which are geared towards the US and Canadian curricula.

Since the mid-1990s, there has been an increasing incidence of students taking SAT exams after the CXC examinations to enable entry into US universities.

The most recent initiative is the College of Science, Technology and Applied Arts of Trinidad and Tobago, which brings together eight tertiary institutions. Almost any subject or course is available in this significant educational programme which is aimed at students who may not have attained suitable CXC exam passes or 'A' Levels.

The other major tertiary educational establishment in Trinidad and Tobago is the University of the West Indies which is situated in St Augustine and is one of the University's three autonomous campuses.

F. KHAN

B. ANTON

Committed to the health of the nation

Dr Austin Trinidade

Arima Regional Hospital

HEALTH care in Trinidad and Tobago is provided through two parallel systems: the public sector, which is free to all citizens and residents of Trinidad and Tobago, and the private sector, which operates on a fee-paying basis.

The public sector health service is administered by five regional Health Authorities and is delivered from strategically situated health centres that are responsible for primary health care. The major hospitals provide secondary and tertiary care. Primary care within the private sector is provided at the offices of family practitioners. Specialists offer secondary and tertiary care from their own private practices and most of these specialists are associated with at least one of the medical centres situated in Port of Spain or San Fernando.

Maternal and child health, immunisation, chronic disease and dental clinics are held at health centres throughout the country. The centres are run by Primary Care Physicians assisted by district nurses and pharmacists. Several of these centres also offer dental care. Secondary care is available at any of the five hospitals in each of the regions.

The largest hospital is the 1,000-bed Port of Spain General in the capital. The San Fernando General in Trinidad's industrial capital has 800 beds. Both of these hospitals offer all the major medical specialities and sub-specialities. They are staffed by highly trained US and UK-trained specialists. Ancillary services are also available.

The Eric Williams Medical Sciences Complex at Mount Hope serves the central region. Apart from being a service hospital, it also offers tertiary services such as open-heart surgery and transplant surgery. This complex is also the teaching hospital for the Faculty of Medical Sciences of the University of the West Indies. Nearby is the Mount Hope Maternity Hospital, a referral centre for problem obstetric cases.

The Sangre Grande District Hospital serves the eastern region and has limited specialist services. More difficult cases are transferred to one of the major hospitals.

The Tobago Regional Hospital is in Scarborough and offers the four major disciplines, with all other cases referred to Trinidad.

Public sector health services also provide a mental hospital, a radiotherapy centre and a thoracic hospital. The five Regional Hospitals provide 24-hour Accident and Emergency services.

Health care in the Private Sector at primary level is delivered out of the practices of General (Family) Practitioners. Several large companies provide separate health services for their employees. One of the best examples is at Petrotrin, the National Oil Company. Not only does it

J. BROWNE

Port of Spain General Hospital

have a medical centre for primary care, but also a hospital staffed by specialists contracted by the company.

Most specialists at the major hospitals also have private practices and patients who attend their consulting rooms can opt to have their care administered at one of the excellent medical centres situated in the north or south of Trinidad.

These centres include the St Clair Medical Centre in Port of Spain, the Seventh Day Adventists Community Hospital in Cocorite, west Trinidad, Medical Associates in Tunapuna in the east, the Southern Medical Clinic, and the Victoria Nursing Home and Surgi-Med Clinic in San Fernando. Patients can expect top class care at these facilities, which provide plush comfort, highly trained specialists and state-of-the-art equipment. All facilities require a fee for service and accept all major medical insurance.

The Emergency Services continue to undergo a major overhaul. A full-scale National Ambulance Service, with trained paramedics, is being introduced with the assistance of the Government of Nova Scotia in Canada. This service will be fully operational in the year 2000.

Public Sector health services are administered jointly by the Ministry of Health and the five Regional Health Authorities. The Ministry is largely responsible for Health policy, whereas the Authorities manage the health facilities in each of region.

A complement to traditional medicine

Raymond Ramcharitar

Mount Hope Medical Complex and Dental School

THE prescription of cure-all herbs, plant roots and leaves, and aromatics dispensed by shamans or old women with heads tied with mysterious looking cloths might seem to be the stuff of bad comedy; but in Trinidad, the shamans might have the last laugh.

Those same practices - herbalism, aromatherapy, crystal healing - have become a part of homeopathy, alternative methods of healing which the Western world has been rediscovering over the last decade or two.

Trinidad has the advantage of retaining its complement of the traditional herbalists - men and women who claim to have retained medicinal secrets from their Amerindian, African and Indian ancestors - alongside a growing retinue of MDs who practice homeopathic medicine. Further swelling the ranks of non-traditional lifestyle groups are chapters of several major alternative spiritual movements.

It is possible to find representatives of Transcendental Meditation, Reiki, Raja Yoga, Aryuveda and Eckankar in the local phone book. A few ashrams (places of meditation) like the Blue Star Ashram exist, and are run by home-grown Eastern-styled gurus, and psychics. Yesenia Adams, a local psychic, even has a radio show.

There is no formal recognition of these activities, and advertising is done usually by reference. For the person wishing a more formal approach to holism, Dr Hari Ramnarine is acknowledged to be the leading local practitioner. Dr Ramnarine's Ishtara Centre in the central town of Chaguanas offers as complete a range of homeopathic treatments including herbs, sound therapy, chromatherapy, electronic acupuncture, Voll testing, and Bach Flower Essence therapy, using up-to-date equipment.

Dr Ramnarine has been practising alternative medicine since the early 1980s, after he completed his formal medical training at the University of the West Indies. At the time, German doctors were beginning to explore alternative techniques of medical treatments and combining them with traditional Western methods. Dr Ramnarine was the among the first non-Germans to share in this knowledge.

The appeal of this type of treatment is that it treats the whole person, not just symptoms of disease. "When a person is sick, it's not just his body, but his mind and spirit too. Healing should take all that into account," he says.

Apart from his practice, Dr Ramnarine speaks regularly at seminars at home and abroad, and conducts yearly holistic retreats

F. KHAN

San Fernando General Hospital

in Trinidad and Tobago which guide participants through meditation, philosophy, and dietary instruction. Dr Ramnarine is one of a few local doctors who has a formal office practice.

Other medical doctors who practice homeopathic medicine include Dr Johnny Siu Chong and Dr Carol Bhaggan-Khan. There is no formal body which incorporates these practitioners, nor is there any licensing arrangement except that any doctors must be licensed by the Trinidadian medical board. However, the situation is changing, says Dr Ramnarine. In 1998, the Food and Drug Licensing Authority included some homeopathic drugs on its approved list of medicinal drugs.

The lack of licensing or organisation belies the numbers of the practitioners who advertise mainly through word of mouth. There are retreats, like the Langmore Foundation, and the Chatham Lodge, which occasionally advertise retreats and seminars.

But for the judicious seeker, it is best to consult one of the MDs who practice homeopathy to ensure activities are conducted with due regard for patient/participant well-being.

Sporting success at home and abroad

Vaneisa Baksh

'Mr Solo', the 1999 winner of the The Great Race

AS a former colony of the British Empire, Trinidad and Tobago was introduced to the quintessential English gentleman's game of cricket, as were the other West Indian islands in the British domain. Eventually, as one analyst said, these island nations took the game and refined it beyond the boundaries of English imagination.

Trinidad and Tobago has provided a profound contribution in the development and creation of the distinctly West Indian style of cricket. The country may not have produced batsmen en masse like Barbados, with maestros like Sir Garfield (Gary) Sobers, Frank Worrell, Clyde Walcott and Everton Weekes, but it has produced men whose global impact on the game is indisputable.

Brian Lara, the current captain of the West Indies team, is ranked as one of the greatest batsmen of all time, having broken Sir Garfield Sobers' 365-run record in 1994 with a memorable innings of 375 in Antigua. His batting has left the cricket world breathless. Sonny Ramadhin was one of the first great bowlers to emerge from the West Indies, and also one of the first Indian-Trinidadians to make his mark. Ramadhin, who emerged in Test cricket in 1950, was paired with Alf Valentine. They became famous the world over as 'Ram and Val', the 'spin twins'. Ramadhin's Test career lasted a decade, from 1950 to 1960, and he played in 43 Test matches claiming 158 wickets. His slow spin and his ability to mask the leg cutter or his off-spin, baffled batsmen who had become used to the pace of the West Indies attack.

"Critics of a sociological turn of mind had proved that we were a nation which naturally produced fast bowlers, when in 1950 Ram and Val, both under twenty-one, produced the greatest slow-bowling sensation since the South African team of 1907. We are moving too fast for any label to stick," wrote CLR James in *Beyond a Boundary*.

CLR James is yet another of the republic's significant contributors to world cricket. His writings on the subject surpassed all that hitherto appeared, notably for their breadth, depth and erudition. They changed perceptions of the game forever.

Learie Constantine was another to play a distinguished part in the sport. Apart from his cricket talents, he was a prolific writer on the game and was published more than any other writer on the subject. His 1933 biographical account, *Cricket and I*, stimulated discussion on the discrimination against Black cricketers. Pelham "Plum" Warner, the MCC president in 1950, was born in Trinidad and he campaigned against the exclusion of Black cricketers from the West Indies team. He believed that cricket should, "symbolise social progress and justice,

Opposite page
Top - Cricket at the Queen's Park Oval
Bottom - The last Derby race at the Queen's Park Savannah

N. NORTON

N. NORTON

Chaguaramas Golf Course

Opposite page
Top - Marathon race
Bottom - Body building competition

and not the endemic racial oppression and class alienation that was challenged by radical socialist and anti-imperial insurgents."

There were several other cricketers from these shores who have shone brightly. Gerry Gomez, Jeffrey Stollmeyer and George John were among several to have made large contributions to this country's most beloved sport.

Cricket in Trinidad and Tobago is considered the 'king' of the sports, but others are now vying for the crown. These 'pretenders' include football (soccer), athletics, golf, horse racing, boxing, hockey, tennis, rugby and snooker.

Trinidadian-born Austin Jack Warner, Vice-President of FIFA, football's world governing body, has done a great deal to address the substantial and burgeoning local interest of this popular sport. There has also been vigorous campaigning to get some of its superstar players back to Trinidad and Tobago to boost the country's chances towards qualifying for the World Cup Finals. They include Tobago-born Dwight Yorke - Manchester United's £12.6 million star striker - goalkeeper Shaka Hislop, Russell Latapy, David Nakhid and Stern John. Their presence in the national team will surely propel Trinidadian football onto the world stage.

In track and field, Ato Boldon heads the current list of world-class Trinidadian athletes. He won the World Championship 200m gold in 1997, after winning the bronze medal at the 1996 Olympic Games in Atlanta. He continues a lineage of sterling sprinters, following in the footsteps of McDonald Bailey and Hasely Crawford, the 1976 Montreal Olympics 100m champion.

Horse racing has long been a great feature of Trinidad and Tobago's

GOLF

Stephen Ames was victorious in the Lyons Open Golf Tournament in 1993 and the Benson & Hedges Open in England in 1996. The following year he achieved fifth place in the British Open at Royal Troon. He was also third in US PGA qualifying tournament in Florida in 1998.

J. BROWNE

J. BROWNE

J. BROWNE

Rugby

sporting calendar. There are numerous derbys throughout the year, especially at Easter and Christmas. The 'Caribbean Classic' has entrants from the entire Caribbean region and is the country's major horse race.

Golf, too, has taken off in a big way, with two major golf courses in Trinidad - the 18-hole St Andrews Golf Club in Maraval, and the nine-hole Chaguaramas public golf course. There is also the world famous 18-hole golf course at the Mount Irvine Bay Hotel in Tobago. The islands aim to increase their tourism portfolios, and are focusing on creating additional golf courses and tournaments. One of the current competitions staged is the Caribbean Junior Golf Championship, a junior version of the Hoerman Cup. It is held each year in Trinidad and Tobago and the winners go on to play at the South American championships, from which the eventual winners proceed to the finals of the Junior World Championship.

Trinidad and Tobago's location at the southern-most tip of the Caribbean island chain has made it an ideal port for pleasure boats and for the development of water sports. Powerboat racing is based at Chaguaramas and reaches its zenith with the annual DuMaurier Great Race Classic in August. The race, which traces a course from Trinidad to Tobago, was inaugurated in 1969 by the Trinidad Yacht Club in Bayshore to promote circuit racing. In those early days, the winners cruised in at a mere 25 mph. Now, and with many international competitors, the boats reach speeds of up to 100 mph.

There are more leisurely and less competitive pursuits in Trinidad and Tobago. These include scuba diving, swimming, surfing and fishing. However, for a truly different type of sport, a trip to Tobago's Heritage Festival will reveal the most unusual event of crab racing!

B. ANTON

Drag racing at Wallerfield

N. NORTON

Trinidad and Tobago Yachting Association races in Tobago

B. ANTON

Show jumping at Queen's Park Savannah

'Red Day', a celebration of football unity

SWIMMING
Cerian Gibbes was one of the top swimmers in the Central American and Caribbean Games (CAC) setting six records in the regional competitions. She was the youngest swimmer, at thirteen years-old, to qualify for the Olympic Games in Atlanta in 1996 where she competed in the 100m breaststroke, the 200m breaststroke and the 50m freestyle.

CYCLING
Cyclist Gene Samuel was a double gold medallist in the Central American and Caribbean Games in the kilo and sprints. He has won eight medals at the Pan-American Games, including three gold medals, and he was a bronze medal winner at the 1991 World Championships.

Learie Constantine

Learie Constantine was 21 years-old when he became a member of the West Indies cricket team that toured England in 1923. His all-round ability delighted spectators from then onwards and throughout a career in which he amassed more than a thousand runs and over one hundred wickets. He was the first West Indies cricketer to score a century in a first class match against an English county side - Northants.

This outstanding cricketer also wrote many books on the game and about his own involvement in cricket, including *Cricket and I*, written in collaboration with CLR James in 1933, *Cricket in the Sun* (1946), *Cricket Crackers* (1949), *Cricketers' Carnival* (1950), and *The Changing Face of Cricket* in 1950 with Denzil Batchelor.

As one of the many players who suffered from the effects of discrimination in the West Indies team, he championed the cause of selection by merit, writing in *Cricket in the Sun* that, "Until players and captains are considered on their merits by a justice blind to the colour of their skins, the West Indies will never take a place in Test match cricket commensurate with the skill of individual West Indian exponents."

A lawyer and diplomat, Learie Constantine served as Special Ambassador to the United Nations, was a Minister in the Trinidad and Tobago Government, and he became the nation's first Ambassador to the Court of St James. He was honoured with a Knighthood, and made a Lord.

A park in his hometown of Tunapuna bears his name, and it is now the home to many of the country's budding cricketers.

J. BROWNE

Basketball at the Besson Street Sports Centre

J. BROWNE

Archery at Chaguaramas

Ellis "Puss" Achong

The originator of the 'Chinaman' bowling delivery in cricket (the left-hander's mirror image of the right-arm leg-break), Ellis "Puss" Achong was the only cricketer of Chinese origin to play for the West Indies.

History recalls the naming of that special delivery in a match against England at Old Trafford in 1933. Walter Robbins exclaimed, after being bowled by Achong, "Fancy being out to a bloody Chinaman!", to which Learie Constantine replied, "Do you mean the bowler or the ball?"

Born in 1904, Ellis Achong, who acquired the nickname "Puss" when playing national football in the 1920s, made his Test debut in 1930 in the second Test against England at the Queen's Park Oval. He went on to play in a further five Tests with the West Indies team.

In 1935, Achong moved to England where he played for Rochdale and Heywood. He claimed no fewer than 1600 wickets up to 1951, and in 1952 he returned to Trinidad. He died in Port of Spain on 29 August 1986.

Sonny Ramadhin

CLR James wrote, while attending the West Indies tour of England in 1950: "Contrary to all expectations, the most striking successes were the two slow bowlers, one twenty in April, the other twenty in May. Ramadhin from Trinidad (he had played only two first-class matches) spun the ball both ways and batsmen seemed unable to detect his changes. (Alf) Valentine from Jamaica... could get more spin from a sound wicket than any left-hander playing. The two of them bowled West Indies to victory in three Tests out of four."

Sonny Ramadhin was born in rural Trinidad in 1929, and became immortalised during his cricket career in song and prose as one of the 'spin twins', 'Ram and Val' (Sonny Ramadhin and Alf Valentine).

In 1950, he topped the tour averages, and his right-arm spin cast him as one of the world's most remarkable bowlers. In the second Test alone, he took eleven wickets for 152 runs.

Throughout the 1950s, Ramadhin mesmerised the cricket world with his superb bowling against Australia in 1951/52, India in 1952/53, and England in 1953/54 where he was the leading wicket-taker (23 wickets) in the five-match Test series.

In New Zealand in 1956, he took six wickets for 23 runs, but the best was to come in the following year when he took seven wickets for 49 runs in the first Test against England at Edgbaston.

By the end of that decade, his formidable career was coming to a close. After playing in 43 Tests and tucking 158 wickets up his always buttoned sleeves, he played his last two Test matches against Australia in the 1960/61 tour.

Hasely Crawford

As a child, Hasely Crawford was small and slightly built - some would say skinny - but he was fast. When he was eight years-old, he caught the eye of a member of the Brooklyn Sports Club in Trinidad and was encouraged to join. He trained hard, and made the national team in 1970 for the Central American and Caribbean Games in Panama, where he achieved fifth place in the 100m and won a bronze medal in the 4 x 400m relay. Later that year, he won another bronze medal in the 100m at the Commonwealth Games in Scotland.

J. HERBERT/ALLSPORT

Brian Lara

In 1972, he reached the 100m final at the Olympic Games in Munich, but was forced to retire from the race just moments out of the blocks with a hamstring injury.

At the Pan-American Games in 1975, he was second in the 100 metres and the following year he finally achieved gold at the Olympic Games in Montreal, beating Jamaica's Don Quarrie and Russia's Valeri Borzov. This victory marked the first Olympic gold medal for Trinidad and Tobago.

Brian Lara

Born on 2 May 1969, Brian Lara exploded on to the world cricket stage in spectacular fashion. His first appearance for the West Indies was in Sydney, Australia where he made an outstanding 277 runs, a performance which heralded the arrival of a truly great batsmen.

The cricket world was mesmerised by his devastating talent which reached a pinnacle on 18 April 1994. It was at the Antigua Recreation Ground that spectators watched in amazement as Lara blasted to a 365-run individual Test score against England, a tally which broke the previously held record of 364 runs held by Sir Garfield Sobers for a staggering 36 years. Brian Lara had faced 538 balls in an innings which lasted more than twelve hours.

Eleven days later, he scored 147 runs for his English county side, Warwickshire, against Glamorgan, and by 23 May he had amassed five consecutive first-class centuries. In June the same year, he was in the record books again with a score of 501 runs, which made him the first batsman to cross the 500 mark in a single first class innings.

In 1998, Brian Lara was made captain of the West Indies team.

S. FORSTER/ALLSPORT

Ato Boldon

Ato Boldon

Ato Boldon was born in Trinidad in 1973, but since 1989 he has lived in New York. In 1992, after his Olympic debut in Barcelona, Boldon made history at the World Junior Championships in Seoul, where he won gold medals in both the 100 metres and 200 metres.

In 1995, at the age of twenty-one, he became the youngest 100 metres medallist in the history of the World Championships, winning bronze in Gothenburg. He was a double bronze medallist at the 1996 Olympics with personal best times of 9.9 seconds in the 100 metres, and 19.8 seconds in the 200 metres. After sustaining an injury in the 100 metres final at the World Championships in 1997, Ato Boldon returned four days later to win his first world title in the 200 metres. It was Trinidad and Tobago's first track gold medal for twenty one years.

"Golden Boldon", as he is affectionately known, opened the 1998 season with a 100 metres time of 9.86 seconds (the third fastest ever) and he won gold in the 200 metres at the Goodwill Games, and set a new Commonwealth record for the 100 metres.

S. BAHADUR

Brian Lara, left, Prime Minister Basdeo Panday and his wife, Oma, at a reception held at the Prime Minister's residence to honour Lara's appointment as captain of the West Indies Cricket team

S. BAHADUR

Dwight Yorke receives the key to Port of Spain in 1999 from Mayor John Raphael

Dwight Yorke

Born in Canaan in Tobago on 3 November 1971, Dwight Yorke always dreamed of being a football star.

He played for the national side in the run-up to the 1990 World Cup, but the team failed to get beyond the preliminary stages of the competition.

In 1989, he attracted the attention of English club Aston Villa, who were touring the Caribbean. He was signed for £120,000 and moved to England. While at the club, he scored a total of 99 goals and became the first player to score twenty league goals in one season.

Manchester United were next to express interest in the talented player, and following protracted negotiations, signed the Tobagonian for a record-breaking £12.6 million.

Dwight Yorke was the leading goal-scorer in the 1998/99 season and helped United to an unprecedented 'treble' of victories - Premier League Champions, FA Cup winners, and European Cup winners.

Overleaf
Dwight Yorke

UMBRO
SHARP
UMBRO
UMBRO

Press freedom based on natural expression

Raymond Ramcharitar

AS one of the few Caribbean nations whose constitution explicitly guarantees freedom of the press, folklore in Trinidad and Tobago recalls that the calypsonians were the first and most reliable 'newspapers' - and to many people, they still are. Calypso singers provide a true vox populi, commenting and reporting on everything from King Edward abdicating his throne to the shortcomings of political administrations.

The belief that the bards are more reliable than the newspapers speaks volumes about the scepticism with which many Trinidadians regard their institutions. This attitude was born in a time when the media had few independent representatives, and was controlled by colonial authorities. But things have changed since then. From five newspapers, one television station, and three radio stations in 1989, there are now three daily and eight weekly newspapers, thirteen radio stations and three television stations. Augmenting this are three cable television providers and one satellite broadcaster.

These days, the Trinidadian public is well-informed. Apart from the scepticism, and the differences in orientation of the media, ethnic origin adds a significant flavour to the recipe. The two main groups - African and Indian - and the smaller Chinese, European and Arab communities, have mixed and intermingled to a degree that is unusual in these days of ethnic polarisation. The result is a society where many influences - ethnicity, education, religion, politics, and socio-economic standing - contribute to the formation of opinions. Members of each group have a place for their opinions, and they make full use of it.

The *Trinidad Guardian* and the *Daily Express* newspapers, the oldest in the country, tend to conservatism. The *Express* is a tabloid and the *Guardian* is the only broadsheet in the country, but apart from a tendency to liberalism by the *Express*, their philosophies are similar. They support a belief in God, morality, democracy and generally uphold the values of the middle and mercantile classes. By contrast, *Newsday*, a newspaper launched in 1993, with its garish front pages and eye for the demotic, appeals to the working people and is the best selling daily.

A few of the weekly newspapers (*Punch*, *Showtime*, and *Dil*) are dedicated to entertainment. Mostly, though, the weeklies are acknowledged experts on the racier and more sordid side of life. They frequently give counter-versions of the stories reported in the dailies, or go where other papers fear to tread - the private lives of leading citizens, for example. The virtue of justice is tested most by papers like the weekly *TnT Mirror*, whose journalism often looks deeper into political and criminal matters than the dailies care to. Taken as a continuum, from the conservative *Guardian* and *Express*, to the sometimes alarming *Bomb* and *Heat*, there is very little of importance in Trinidad and Tobago which goes unrecorded or viewed from multiple perspectives.

In media matters, Tobago is largely left to its own devices. The space given to it in the Trinidadian press is small, and the newspaper, *Tobago News* is devoted to the smaller island's affairs, along with one radio station, Tambrin 92.1 FM.

Players on the Trinidadian airwaves are more numerous, and the radio stations pitch to every conceivable market - Caribbean and US popular music, Christian music, East Indian music, news and commentary (talk radio), Trinidadian music, dub and dancehall, adult contemporary, oldies, sport, and various permutations of all genres which are constantly in the throes of fierce competition.

The least developed area of the media-scape is television. Of the three stations - CCN TV6, TTT and TIC - the latter two are government-controlled. This means a fair share of government programming, mostly documentaries, but otherwise, all rely mainly on US programming.

Given the country's rich and vibrant ethnic and social mix, the outsider might be forgiven for believing there is material aplenty for soap operas and television dramas. While local novelists draw freely from the treasure trove of stories, economics usually prevents film and television producers from doing the same.

Predictably, in such a diverse milieu, there are the usual frissons and frictions. In the last five years government criticism of the press has increased. There have been accusations from the government and the population of bias and laxity in fulfilling their function, and, in the words of Prime Minister Basdeo Panday, a predilection for, "lies, half-truths and innuendoes". Unlike elsewhere, though, the resolutions are remarkably civilised. The very response to the criticism - hot debate - has underlined the resiliency and protean nature of freedom of the press in Trinidad and Tobago.

The Express newspaper in its Sunday opinion section places side by side Selwyn Cudjoe, an Afrocentric apologist, and Kamal Persad, an Indocentric apologist. Both men essay partisan ethnocentric views, which often include condemnations of each other's political views and groups. However, they do so with lucid, rational arguments, occasional rantings, but never ethnic slurs. And neither has there ever been ethnically-motivated violence in Trinidad and Tobago.

Trinidadians lovingly accept the grammatical infelicities of the radio disc jockeys - many styled upon their US counterparts. They also, not so lovingly, tolerate the solecisms and occasional factual faux pas in the press. The reporting is heavily oriented toward bald facts, and little space is given to affairs of art, literature or cultural analysis.

An understanding of the spirit of press freedom is alive and well in Trinidad and Tobago, so much so that the country has exported the idea. Ken Gordon, chairman of the Caribbean Communications Network group, has been instrumental in helping local investors to set up newspapers and television stations in virtually every Caribbean territory during the last quarter century. Mr Gordon was also influential in the setting up of CANA, the Caribbean News Agency, an indigenous organisation which took the responsibility for providing wire reports from the foreign-controlled Reuters and AFP agencies.

Opposite
The press in Trinidad and Tobago

Sunday PUNCH
The Love Paper $2.50 {VAT Incl.}
ISSUE No. 736
BLAST
$2.50
(VAT INCLUSIVE)
LARGEST READERSHIP OF ANY NEWSPAPER IN T&T
the independent
the bomb
CUREPE: TRINIDAD
$2.00
T&T MIRROR
THE SUPER PAPER
Texaco up station
Trinidad Guardian
http://www.guardian.co.tt
THE GUARDIAN OF DEMOCRACY
Daily Express
The National Newspaper of Trinidad & Tobago
NOW $1
Sunday Guardian
26454 ESTABLISHED SEPTEMBER 2, 1917
Saturday Express
Sunday Newsday
$2
DISPLAY YOUR NEWSDAY & WIN $1,000 EVERY DAY!
Sunday Express
The National Newspaper of Trinidad & Tobago
Trinidad & Tobago's
Newsday
The People's Newspaper
$1
FREEDOM OF THE PRESS

Diversity in science and technology

Peter Hannomansingh

R. COOK

Control Room at the Caribbean Methanol Plant in Couva

IN 1793, the Spanish astronomer Don Cosmo Damien Churruca established for the first time an accurate meridian in the New World. This he did from an observatory in Laventille, near Port of Spain. When he returned to Spain later that year, Don Cosmo completed his task by observing the star 'Aldebaran' from Cadiz. Thereby, he was able to link the Old World with the New World and establish an absolute longitude, the first one so fixed in the hemisphere.

Don Cosmo literally put the once neglected colony of Trinidad on the map. With a population of a nearly fifteen thousand in 1793, Trinidad was still a frontier zone.

The plantation system, which could dominate a society so completely, developed quite late in Trinidad. This, as much as anything, provided the spaces in the economy for other activities. It was in Trinidad after all, that disputably the first successful oil well was drilled.

In 1857, two years before Edwin Drake struck oil in Pennsylvania, the Merrimac Oil Company is reported to have found oil in the vicinity of the Pitch Lake at La Brea. Historians have a divided opinion of this event, but it is clear that Trinidad played a pioneering role in the development of the oil industry.

In 1865, Walter Darwent struck oil in Aripero, a village four miles east of La Brea. This effort did not last and Darwent himself died just three years later. Commercial quantities of oil came with the activities of the English investor, Randolph Rust who struck oil in the Guayaguayare area in 1902. Two years later the British government took an interest in oil exploration in Trinidad as it was in the process of converting its navy to oil-powered ships. As a result of prospecting in the area, initiated by the British government, Trinidad Oilfields Ltd was established.

By 1911, Trinidad and Tobago had become a modest producer and exporter of oil with the establishment of a small refinery in Point Fortin.

The oil industry would continue to develop, opening up southern Trinidad and transforming the politics of the country. The industry would in turn become a centre of radical labour politics and which would result in the consolidation of the trade union movement. Ultimately, this would play an important role in the political development of the nation.

After World War II, a new technological invention would emerge indirectly from oil. This time, it would come from the margins of the society. This new invention would transform the cultural landscape

INFORMATION TECHNOLOGY
Information Technology (IT) developed relatively early in Trinidad and Tobago because of the energy sector. A few local software development companies in the energy field have been contracting customers in the United States. Industry analysts estimate that within the next five years approximately forty percent of the population will have personal computers and some 20,000 internet users. There are currently seven internet service providers. Plans are underway for the development of a 1100-acre Science and Technology Park which would house technology-oriented companies and research groups.

R. COOK

6
Miller

R. COOK

Container docks at the harbour in Port of Spain

of the country, and indeed become an important Caribbean icon.

The steelpan was born in the 1940s in the urban village of Laventille, the place where Don Cosmo made his landmark observations. Although seen as a musical instrument, the 'pan', as it is simply called, is by all definitions, a distinct technology. Initially devised from old containers, the ready availability of oil barrels provided a route toward its development from simple percussion into a full orchestral instrument.

From its early development as an ad hoc accompaniment to rival street bands of the Carnival festival, the pan is now in the hands of apprenticed professionals. Technical research and development has brought a finer sound and greater versatility to the instrument. Research continues not only in Trinidad and Tobago, but as far afield as Switzerland and the United States where the largest factory can be found at Akron, Ohio. There are a number of patents on design and technology coming out of this musical instrument which is a mere half century in the making.

Trinidad and Tobago's pioneering role has continued to the present day with the development of natural gas and heavy industry.

Oil production began to decline in the 1980s, but abundant reserves of natural gas have proven a boon to the economy. As a cheaper and cleaner source of fuel, natural gas provided a basis for lower costs of production in heavy industry. Thus began a policy thrust toward energy-intensive industrialisation which resulted in the establishment of the first steel plant in the English-speaking Caribbean at Point Lisas.

In 1993, the country became host to the world's first iron carbide

A TELEVISUAL FIRST

The first television signal to be transmitted anywhere in the world may have been in the cool Santa Cruz valley in Trinidad. John Logie Baird, a Scotsman escaping the harsh winters of his homeland, came to Trinidad in late 1919 and continued his work in transmitting pictures at the Stollmeyer Estate. The story goes that he succeeded in sending a crude but recognisable picture of a human face from one house to another, a distance of a few hundred feet. Baird later returned to the United Kingdom where it is believed he played a pivotal role in the development of radar technology for the military, some time before its official 'invention'.

F. KHAN

Construction of the WASA Water Treatment Plant (top of picture) at Piarco International Airport

plant. Four years later, a new direct reduced iron plant was sited in Trinidad. The plant, owned by major producers Cliff and Associates, became the first to employ the newly developed Circored technology, leading one government official to forecast the country could become known as the land of alternative steel technology, as well as the land of the steelband.

Along with steel, Trinidad and Tobago has become a lead player in the world in the production of methanol, ammonia and urea. In 1999, the giant Atlantic LNG (liquid natural gas) at Point Fortin became the first 'grassroots' LNG plant to be constructed in the Western hemisphere in thirty years. At an estimated US$1 billion, Atlantic became the single largest investment in the entire Caribbean, putting Trinidad and Tobago firmly on the world LNG map.

Considerable local expertise had developed with the expansion of the economy following the celebrated oil boom of the 1970s. The engineering profession has been well served in this time by the University of the West Indies (UWI). Though best known for its training at undergraduate level, the university has been gradually moving toward greater co-operation with industry and business. There are now at least three important centres of research and technology development located on the campus at St Augustine.

The Caribbean Industrial Research Institute (CARIRI), established by an Act of Parliament in 1981, offers a host of technical support for industry in addition to consultancy services in a variety of fields. CARIRI has been engaged in some degree of indigenous research and development over the years, but more recently has focused its efforts on providing technical services and advice to industry in

YACHT CONSTRUCTION

A pleasure craft service industry has grown rapidly since 1994. Trinidad and Tobago are below the 12th degree parallel and are relatively protected from the ravages of hurricanes in the region. This industry now earns upwards of US$12 million per annum and has also helped to further a pleasure craft construction sector. The country now builds pirogues, power boats, yachts and sports crafts from both fibreglass and locally grown teak. The annual Great Race between the two islands is a power boat affair driven by indigenous know-how.

Bridge construction over the Otoire River in Manzanilla

F. KHAN

HOME-GROWN INNOVATION

Although the spectacular rise of the energy sector has overshadowed activity in other areas of the economy, the country can boast important contributions in agriculture and in the life sciences. The popular aquarium fish known as the 'millions', but more widely known as the guppy was co-discovered by Trinidadian, Lechmere Guppy in 1859. In agriculture, Dr Steve Bennett developed the hardy hybrid known by the colourful name, 'buffalypso'. This tropically adapted cattle species has become important livestock in a number of countries in neighbouring South America. Other important innovations include the patented coconut dehusker and the dwarf pigeon peas plant, a type more amenable to large scale cultivation.

A PASSION FOR COCOA

Trinidad and Tobago is home to the most diverse collection of cocoa in the world. Once a top producer of cocoa, the country is now a leading centre of research for the international industry. The Cocoa Research Unit (CRU) established in 1930, pursues work in selection, breeding, propagation and conservation. Recently, scientists at the CRU recovered ancient strains of cocoa used by the Mayan nobility deep in the Guatemalan rainforests.

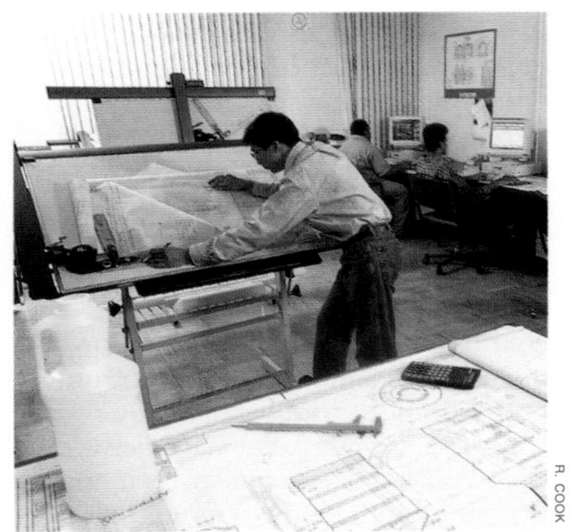
R. COOK

areas such as food technology, microbiology, industrial materials technology, environmental management, and analytical chemistry. CARIRI boasts the only independent petroleum lab in the country and has played a pivotal role in the development of the energy sector in the country.

The Engineering Institute, on the other hand, was the initiative of the UWI in its attempt to provide a formal link between academia and industry. As such, the institute is managed by a board comprising members of the Faculty of Engineering as well as representatives of business and industry. The institute acts as co-ordinator for a number of centres which conduct research and training. The Centre for Energy Studies, for example, has been engaged in research in wind generation as well as other collaborative projects in electric power.

The UWI is also home to the Real Time Systems Group (RTSG), a development research body that operates out of the Faculty of Engineering and which focuses largely on the areas of automation, communications, electronics and information technology. RTSG counts some of the largest corporations in the country among its clients and also serves organisations in other Caribbean territories. Recent projects include the devising of magnetic pick-up methods for the steelpan, the development of energy control networks as well as the work in the design of real time computer systems.

Most of the scientific research and development work funded by the state has historically gone into agriculture and marine sciences. Here, too, the university has played an important role in providing a trained scientific cadre for research in various aspects of the natural sciences. At the beginning of the 1990s, the National Institute of Higher Education, Research, Science and Technology estimated that there were more than 21,000 people employed in occupations of science and technology. This represented some 4.6 per cent of the workforce. This figure can be expected to rise significantly as the number of graduates at the university increases by about eight percent per annum.

One might quip that Trinidad and Tobago's growing technical diversity compliments its cultural diversity. There might be a lesson in there that is yet to be discovered.

Economic stability built on petroleum

Mervyn Crichlow

PETROLEUM in its various forms – asphalt, crude oil and natural gas – helps to make the Republic of Trinidad and Tobago one of the wealthy countries in the Caribbean and Latin American region. It is the main source of government revenue, foreign exchange earnings and the stimulus for economic growth. The nation's petroleum industry is now poised to more effectively deal with the challenges posed by the realities of the international market that impinge upon a small country with finite resources.

Asphalt

Natural asphalt - a complex emulsion of water, gas, bitumen and mineral matter – from the Pitch Lake at La Brea, is used worldwide as a modifier in road and tarmac construction. For over a century it has

Oil rig in the Gulf of Paria

been described as "a unique geographical phenomenon." Sir Walter Raleigh discovered the Pitch Lake in 1595 and the sea-faring Europeans of that era used the asphalt first for caulking ships and a wide range of applications, including its use as lamp oil. The current volume of natural asphalt is ten million tonnes, which equates to over four hundred years of reserves at current extraction rates.

Crude Oil

Walter Darwent, an American engineer, found the first deposits of crude oil at Aripero (about eight miles south of San Fernando) in 1866. More oil (carbon and hydrogen) was discovered three years later in Aripero by Randolph Rust and Edwin Lee Lum. The southern parts of Trinidad proved to be rich in oil-bearing rocks and many companies were set up by British and American firms. Serious oil drilling began in 1907, this time in the Point Fortin area.

Exploration in the northern half of Trinidad and in Tobago was not successful. Exploration for marine oil began in 1954 off the west coast (Soldado Fields). This was followed in the late 1960s by major discoveries off Trinidad's east coast by the Pan American Trinidad Oil Company. Companies operating in Trinidad and Tobago's hydrocarbon industry read as a veritable *Who's Who* of modern industry. To date, approximately 2.6 billion barrels of oil have been produced from oilfields both on and off-shore.

Natural Gas

Natural gas has come a long way since the Amoco Trinidad Oil Company made the first major gas discovery in 1968 off the south-east coast of Trinidad. Since 1995, however, gas production has exceeded crude oil in terms of barrels of energy equivalent. This trend is expected to continue.

The Petroleum Company of Trinidad and Tobago (Petrotrin), is engaged in gas exploration and production and is gearing up to become active in downstream petrochemical manufacture. Gas-based industries (the petrochemical subsector) currently provides over three thousand direct jobs, and under stable market conditions generates over US$2 billion in annual revenues. The ambition of the National Gas Company is to establish Trinidad and Tobago as a major player in the global natural gas business.

J. BROWNE

LNG, Ammonia and Methanol

Trinidad and Tobago continues to set world standards in the hydrocarbon industry. In 1999, five companies involved in gas supply, processing and LNG marketing, joined in partnership to establish at Point Fortin, the world's largest single-train (three million tonnes a year) Liquefied Natural Gas facility - Atlantic LNG. This LNG plant builds on the country's position as the sole LNG export plant in the whole of the Latin American and Caribbean region, and the second in the entire western hemisphere.

Trinidad and Tobago is also the world's largest ammonia exporter and by the end of 1999, the world's largest methanol exporter.

The wave of the future

Reserves of oil and gas could increase over the next three to five years. This is due to the recent award of fifteen production-sharing contracts

Petrotrin refinery at Pointe-a-Pierre

to international companies willing to join resources to share the risks while exploiting business opportunities off Trinidad's east coast.

The wave of the future will see the construction of an aluminium smelter plant at Point Lisas by 2002 and deepening of the natural gas industrial base involving gas-to-liquids technology, the manufacture of ethylene and its derivatives, expansion of ammonia and methanol production as well as expansion of the steel industry.

The fundamental challenge now is to use natural gas to continue to fuel economic and industrial development and at the same time achieve some specific objectives. These include a balanced portfolio of investment with a larger proportion of higher valued downstream activities, facilitation of the growth of ancillary industries as well as the enhancement of local technological capability.

Trinidad and Tobago is well recognised internationally for its attractive investment environment, a fact which has greatly facilitated the country's industrialisation thrust.

The country has many advantages in the competition for foreign investment. Some of these result from the long history of the local hydrocarbon industry, whilst others result from the fact that a wide range of trans-national oil and gas companies are currently operating in the local energy sector.

Petrotrin

The Petroleum Company of Trinidad and Tobago Limited, the integrated State petroleum company, was established in 1993 to manage the substantial petroleum assets and personnel of two State oil companies, Trintoc and Trintopec. The acreage under its control

Pumping oil in Piparo

spans the southern half of Trinidad and includes off-shore acreage on the southern, south-eastern and south-western coasts of Trinidad.

The employees of Petrotrin rank as some of the most experienced and highly trained workforces in the local industry.

Exploration and Production

Petrotrin produces crude oil and some natural gas in the on-shore area of south Trinidad – Palo Seco, Los Bajos, Guapo, Forest Reserve, Quarry, Penal-Barrackpore, Parrylands, Guayaguayare, Tabaquite, Goudron and Morne Diablo/Quinam. Off-shore the company's operations are confined to the north-east coast of Galeota Point which is located at the south-east of Trinidad. Petrotrin controls two thirds of Trinmar, the largest marine operator in Trinidad and Tobago in terms of the number of producing wells and structures that it maintains.

Refining and Marketing

Petrotrin owns and operates the country's only refinery that, over the years, has been expanded and modernised. This refinery, with a capacity of 160,000 barrels a day, is located at Pointe-a-Pierre. It manufactures petroleum products – Liquefied Petroleum Gases (LPG), Aviation Gasoline, Motor Gasoline, Kerosene/Avjet, Gas Oil/No 2 Fuel Oil, Lube Oils, Fuel Oils, Sulphur and Bitumen - for local consumption and for export to regional and international markets. The former Point Fortin Refinery site has been transformed into a terminalling operation.

Petrotrin has reorganised for higher performance and is fired with a vision to become, within ten years, a pacesetter refinery in the region. Ultimately, Petrotrin hopes its refinery will become the preferred supplier in the Caribbean and Latin America competing in profitability, quality, efficiency, cost, safety and environmental excellence with the top refineries of the world.

Opportunities continue to exist for foreign investors to participate as joint venture partners in all aspects of Petrotrin's operations – exploration and production, refining and marketing of petroleum products as well as support services. The company recognises that today's competitiveness can be eroded by fundamental shifts in the business environment and consequently strategies are in place to generate new exploration activity through the mechanism of joint venture partnerships. Strategies are in place to upgrade the refinery and increase refining margins so that the company can take its place among the top performers.

Trinidad and Tobago, with its stable economy, is a prime candidate for investment in energy projects and Petrotrin looks forward to doing business with interested parties as the petroleum industry continues its rapid expansion.

World class industry at Point Lisas

Angela Gouveia

SITUATED on the central west coast of Trinidad, is Point Lisas Industrial Estate and Port, a world class industrial complex and multi-purpose harbour. Using natural gas as a feedstock and energy source, this area has played a central role in the economic success of Trinidad and Tobago.

Point Lisas Industrial Port Development Corporation Limited (PLIPDECO) is the landlord of this 860-hectare site, which includes the general cargo facilities.

The area was initially developed in the 1970s to utilise the natural gas reserves which provided in excess of 500 million cubic feet a day. By the year 2000, it is estimated that gas consumption will be in the region of 1.1 billion cubic feet a day. This does not include the 460 million cubic feet a day required to support the liquefied natural gas (LNG) project along the south coast of the island.

PLIPDECO currently has ninety tenants whose products range from ammonia, methanol and steel, to breakfast cereals, cheese and service industries.

Industries are attracted to the area because of the available facilities - piped natural gas, electricity power station, fibre optic telecommunications, potable water, excellent location and an efficient multi-purpose harbour.

Ammonia production and processing is represented by Canadian

N. NORTON

Powergen power plant at Point Lisas

Plipdeco

Potash Corporation of Saskatchewan (PCS), one of the largest ammonia complexes in the world which also produces granular urea; Hydro Agri Limited, owned by Norwegian company Norsk Hydro; Tringen, owned by the Trinidad and Tobago Government; Norsk Hydro, and the US-owned, Farmland Miss Chem Limited. The current annual production is approximately 3.8 million tonnes, making Trinidad and Tobago one of the world's top three exporters of ammonia.

There are four methanol production plants owned by local company, Clico Energy, and Ferostaal AG of Germany. Total annual production stands at 2.2 million metric tonnes. However, it is projected that by December 2000, following the addition of US-owned Titan Methanol, production will increase by 830,000 metric tonnes. This will make Trinidad and Tobago the largest producer and exporter of methanol worldwide.

Caribbean Ispat Limited, a subsidiary of the International Mittal Group of India, produces 2.3 million tonnes of direct reduced iron (DRI), 830,000 tonnes of steel billets, and 650,000 metres of coiled wire rods. A new steel project by US-owned Cliffs and Associates is being commissioned to produce 500,000 tonnes of hot briquetted iron (HBI) annually.

A natural gas liquids plant, owned by Conoco, Pan West and the National Gas Company, currently extracts butane, propane and gasoline from 860 million cubic feet of natural gas every day. This is expected to increase to over one billion cubic feet by the year 2000, with the arrival of the Titan Methanol Project and the Cliffs and Associates HBI plant.

N. NORTON

PLIPDECO/MICHAEL BONAPARTE STUDIOS

Point Lisas shipping terminal

PCS Nitrogen is the largest ammonia complex in the western hemisphere

Corporation with a passion for excellence

The head offices of Trinidad and Tobago Insurance Ltd (TATIL) in Port of Spain. Built in 1963, this twelve-storey building was the country's first high-rise

THE Ansa McAl Group of Companies is one of the largest enterprises in the Caribbean. The group's headquarters are in Trinidad and Tobago and its workforce of about 6,000 people is spread through Guyana, Barbados, St Kitts, Jamaica and the United States.

The diversity of its operations embraces the brewing of the Caribbean's most popular beer, Carib, the manufacturing of glass containers, paint, chlorine and other chemical products, clay blocks, dies, steel and aluminium windows, matches, flexible plastic packaging materials and moulded products and stationery. In addition to its manufacturing operations, the group markets and distributes food, household goods, pharmaceuticals, cosmetics, liquor, and biomedical items. It is a leader in the supply of office and household furniture, information technology, oilfield, petrochemical and industrial supply and service, and offers travel and shipping services.

It has the largest automobile dealerships in the Caricom region, owns two newspapers and four radio frequencies accounting for over 30% of radio listenership in Trinidad and Tobago. It has substantial interests in real estate development and is prominent in the insurance field. It holds the majority interest in the Ansa Finance and Merchant Bank in Trinidad and Tobago and, in Barbados, operates a finance company.

Mindful of its obligations to the needs and aspirations of the society it serves, the Ansa McAl Foundation was formed and funded by an appropriation of 1% of the Group's total profit before tax. From 1992 to 1998, it contributed $18 million to the foundation. These funds were used for a wide range of social services, which included the construction of, and financial support for, the Ansa McAl Psychological Research Centre at the University of the West Indies.

The group has generously supported cultural expression in Trinidad and Tobago in all its forms including dance, music and sport. In this latter area, the group sponsored the West Indies Cricket Team for the 1999 World Cup and the tour of England in the year 2000.

Ansa McAl traces its origin from the end of the 19th Century and the initiatives of two entrepreneurs. The first was George Alston who, in 1881, established a small firm (Alstons) that bought and exported cocoa. At that time, Trinidad was the second largest cocoa producer in the world. Charles McEnearney was the other who, in 1919, won the franchise for Ford and introduced the motor car to Trinidad and Tobago. McEnearney and Alstons combined forces in 1969, and in

Concrete products at Bestcrete, part of the Ansa McAl group

1976 McEnearney acquired the minority shareholding of Alstons which finally consummated the union of the two groups and led to the name 'McEnearney Alstons'.

In 1986, the Ansa McAl Group, founded in the 1940s by another outstanding entrepreneur, Anthony Sabga, became the major stockholder in McEnearney Ltd.

In 1992, the McEnearney Alstons Group formally adopted the name Ansa McAl which reflects the present ownership structure of the group in which Ansa is the majority stockholder.

In this way, one of the Caribbean's largest, most diversified business groups was built. Throughout the history of what is today Ansa McAl, the common threads have been integrity, enterprise and growth. It was the first to start indigenous operations in brewing, insurance, radio, edible oil refining, glass and clay products manufacturing. It sold the first BWIA airline ticket and constructed the country's first office block. Its match factory dates from 1887, its shipping agency from 1905 and the newspaper from 1917.

From the early years Ansa McAl has spearheaded industrialisation. From inception, its founders appreciated the need for expansion and the capital to underwrite it. For this reason, it became a Public Company in 1947. Prior to 1962, its shares were quoted on the London Stock exchange. In 1990 its $100 million Bond Issue was fully subscribed and was the first such private sector placement to be publicly issued.

Throughout its more that one hundred years, Ansa McAl has been conscious of the importance of providing value for those who do business with it, of the need to create new wealth to achieve long term benefits for its stockholders and employees. It is of and for the Caribbean. It tries to be an exemplary corporate citizen and an example to others by playing a significant part in the contribution the private sector must make in building the region. It is committed to continuously evolving to satisfy its markets and to strive to be the best in whatever it does.

Ansa McAl enters the year 2000 with the confidence, the vision, the zest and the passion that has through the years characterised its quest for excellence.

The High Commission for Canada is situated at Maple House. Construction was completed in 1996

Clay products manufactured at Abel which is part of the Ansa McAl group

Bayside Towers is a luxury complex of two hundred apartments which dominates the entrance to Trinidad's north-western peninsula

A model of financial growth and success

Raymond Ramcharitar

TRINIDAD and Tobago is, perhaps, the only Caribbean nation - and one of the few countries in the developing world - which appears to be winning the development battle.

In the early 1970s, the islands, and their Caribbean neighbours, were busily grappling with the problems of newly acquired independence. Freed of sterling, the exchange rate was fixed to the US dollar, and the dependence on a single primary export (petroleum) was considered in no danger of ending in the near future. Growth was low, unemployment was high, foreign exchange was scarce.

Then came the OPEC oil shocks of the 1970s, and, as a result of increased revenues between 1974 to 1982, the nation's economy experienced an average annual growth of more than six percent. Government revenues sky-rocketed providing funding for development projects which led to a dramatic drop in unemployment.

The financial sector also grew and diversified and the numbers of finance companies, merchant banks, and trust and financial companies, doubled from eleven in 1974 to twenty-two by 1978.

However, by 1980 the country's appetite for foreign consumables and travel had, despite the fixed exchange rate and tight controls, sent the economy into recession from 1983 to 1984. Foreign debts and fiscal deficits had risen, oil production fell and the currency was devalued. A major oil price increase was implemented to stem the decline.

In the mid-1980s, the International Monetary Fund (IMF) was brought in to appease foreign creditors, and for the next ten years, the agency dictated the country's economic planning, monetary and fiscal policy. The currency was again devalued and many non-banking financial institutions collapsed.

But Trinidad and Tobago, as a nation, emerged from this uncertain period free from major debt and ready to move forward. By 1997, foreign exchange controls were removed and the currency regained its stability.

Today, the financial sector is possibly one of the most internationally integrated in the Caribbean. By 1999, there were six commercial banks including two foreign-owned banks - Intercommercial (India) and Citibank (USA). There are ten finance companies and merchant banks, six mortgage and trust companies, 356 credit unions, and two development banks. The insurance industry comprises about 46 companies, twenty engaged in life or long-term insurance and twenty-six in general products. These include the specialised institutions Export Credit Insurance Company, the Reinsurance

Port of Spain

Company of Trinidad and Tobago, and the National Insurance Board - a social insurance company whose assets are mainly mortgage-based. The top ten insurance companies control about eighty percent of the industry's assets, and some are part of interlocking conglomerates involved in everything from media to construction.

In addition, there are several local and foreign currency mutual funds, usually attached to the commercial banks. The most successful, and first established, Unit Trust Corporation, guarantees a return on the investment of at least the face value, and averages a return of about ten percent a year - a favourable rate considering that inflation is well below five percent.

The assets of the finance sector in Trinidad and Tobago have grown from $912 million in 1970 to $45,570 million in 1995, and thirty-one companies are now traded in the local stock market. The country's foreign bankability was underlined in September 1999 with a successful Eurobond issue which raised US$230 million.

Ideal climate for a sound investment

Raymond Ramcharitar

Anthurium nursery in Centeno

THE beauty of Trinidad and Tobago is that, unlike other investor destinations, it can accommodate the retiree with the nest egg, or the multi-national corporation with the hundreds of millions with equal facility.

Unusually for the Caribbean, the country's economic mainstay has traditionally been mineral, rather than agricultural or tourist-dependent. Particularly over the last few years, several hundred million US dollars have been pumped into the local oil and petrochemical industries. Ammonia, methanol and steel processing plants have been set up by multi-national companies like Enron, Amoco BP, Exxon, Union Carbide and Farmland Miss Chemicals.

These mirror the traditional investment patterns of the early 1960s. The oil industry was capital intensive, generating hundreds of construction jobs in the early phases. But after construction, the permanent jobs created were few, and the earnings enjoyed by government were mainly from taxation.

The oil windfall was distributed through the society in the form of high-paying civil service jobs, free public health and education. As a result of this, a large middle class burgeoned, with the requisite consumer patterns and expectations.

At the same time, small-scale, low technology industry like light manufacturing and food processing developed. This added to Trinidad and Tobago's other attributes, natural and otherwise, make it receptive to other smaller scale business ventures.

According to the Tourism and Industrial Development Corporation's (TIDCO's) investment guide, "... policies will focus on strategies for development which expand and promote employment opportunities, domestic food security, nutrition, private investment, sustainable management of land, water forest and marine resources."

As an awareness of the necessity for curtailing foreign spending has spread through the society, successive governments have actively supported and encouraged development of these sectors. There are tax concessions, subsidies, provision of sites like Free Zones, assistance and allowances for export-oriented businesses, and a regulative smoothening of bureaucratic procedures.

Despite four separate government administrations over the last twenty years, the fundamental philosophy of encouraging investors into these areas has remained unchanged, and many local and foreign investors have availed themselves of the benefits. But the numbers

F. KHAN

Dairy products manufacturing at Nestle

N. NORTON

Cuatro-maker

F. KHAN

Royal Bank at Brian Lara Promenade and South Quay, Port of Spain

F. KHAN

Courts Furniture and Electrical Superstore in Port of Spain

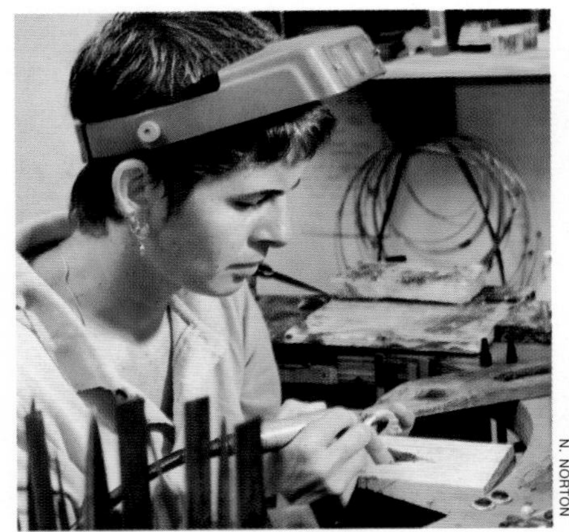

Jewellery-maker

The new headquarters of Gulf Insurance on Tragarete Road in Port of Spain

Republic Bank in Mayaro

have been small (and profits large) perhaps because the needs were not well publicised.

TIDCO was created to meet this need - for information provision and investment promotion - in 1995, and is the main agency through which foreign investors must pass. Its Investment Promotions and Investment Facilitation divisions are equipped to provide prospective investors with all the information necessary - from legislation, to balance of payments statistics, to which sectors are most in need of investment - to make investment decisions.

So, the scope of activity is as protean as the investor's imagination. Starting a small business here might be as simple as a low-technology tattoo shop or a bar, or as high-technology as an Information Technology consultancy service, or as ambitious as a nature resort in Tobago.

Apart from the normal package of facilities the government extends to prospective investors, there are other things which make the island more desirable than any other Caribbean site.

Comprising the workforce of just over 540,000 (according to Price Waterhouse/Coopers) are university graduates, in all disciplines from

Opposite page
Top - Alcoa bauxite transfer station in Chaguaramas
Bottom - Trinidad Cement Ltd., Claxton Bay

F. KHAN

J. BROWNE

CL FINANCIAL

Colonial Life Insurance Company (Trinidad) Limited was founded in 1936 by Trinidad-born Cyril Lucius Duprey. At forty years-old, Duprey had gained considerable experience in life insurance in the United States where he had lived and worked for more than twenty years. The immediate success of his organisation was attributed to the fact that it targeted the working classes or "barefoot man", as they were referred to in those early days.

From the 1950s, CLICO incorporated other financial institutions and made several acquisitions. Now known as CL Financial, the group is extensively diversified throughout Trinidad and Tobago as well as in the Caricom region. This is in keeping with its philosophy of a "boundaryless, learning organisation, engaged in diverse businesses for the enhancement of the quality of life in our communities."

N. NORTON

Fishermen in Mayaro inspect the catch of the day

liberal arts to medical sciences, from the University of the West Indies in St Augustine. There are skilled and semi-skilled labourers, and of the rest, the majority have attained at least a high school education.

The country is also by far the most technically sophisticated in the Caribbean. The telecommunications industry is highly developed, and metropolitan consumer goods - everything from bagels to BMW motor cars - are available.

The nation's secondary schools provide quality education, and many local students acquire scholarships to American universities. There are two private high schools in Port of Spain instituted by the expatriate American and Canadian communities which provide North American and Canadian standard education.

The financial system is the most sophisticated and extensive in the Caribbean. There are six banks whose branches are spread across the country. The number includes banks with at least partial foreign

Opposite page
Top - Cane tractor on a sugar cane plantation in Claxton Bay
Bottom - Yachting basin at Chaguaramas

R. COOK

N. NORTON

HI-LO FOOD STORES

Hi-Lo Food Stores is a chain of supermarkets comprising twenty retail outlets located throughout Trinidad. A subsidiary of Neal & Massy Holdings Limited, the company celebrates its 50th anniversary in the year 2000.

Known as, "The Nation's Favourite Food Store", Hi-Lo is committed to providing a wide variety of goods at competitive prices and with friendly and efficient service.

Carib Brewery

ownership - The Bank of Nova Scotia (Canada), the Intercommercial Bank (India), and Citibank (Trinidad and Tobago) Ltd (USA).

The success of IMF policies under the supervision of the Central Bank has kept inflation at about four percent (1997), brought the debt-service ratio to about ten percent of GDP, and has seen the economy grow for four successive years (1997 figures) according to Price Waterhouse/ Coopers. The rate of exchange is a managed float, which allows the free movement of capital in and out of the country.

As in other countries, the public utilities, health services, and other amenities are adequate and are constantly addressed. The public health system is undergoing restructuring, but there are several privately run medical clinics which are at least as well equipped as any 'Western' country. The public transportation system relies mainly on private taxi and mini-bus operators and, as they say locally, "Everyone gets where they're going."

Chief Brand Products. Chairman and Founder Sayeed Khan started his business in 1957 from what was originally a 'one man show'. Chief Brand Products is now one of the largest manufacturers and exporters of spices and seasonings in the Caribbean

For the investor who has had enough of the fast pace of the consumer society and wishes to invest in a place which is free from the constraints of conventional business, Tobago might be more suitable. Although it is the same country, Trinidad's sister island presents a calmer side. All amenities which exist in Trinidad are available in Tobago, but Tobagonians are less concerned with technology than they are with peace of mind. This means an entirely different set of imperatives for investment. There are several self-contained resorts being constructed which aim at the high-end luxury market, a much more affluent group than the average tourist. This means that once these concerns are up and running, by 2002, Tobago's needs would include non-traditional services, like yacht-marina services, golf course maintenance, imports of cosmetics and spa products, and maintenance services for the many condominiums and villas being constructed now.

A comprehensive information package of the provisions for investment in Trinidad and Tobago is available from consulates and missions throughout the world, or direct from: *TIDCO, 10-14 Philipps Street, Port of Spain, Trinidad. Tel. 623 6022/3, 623 1932/4. Fax. 623 3848. E-mail: tourism-info@tidco.co.tt. Website: www.tidco.co.tt, and, www.investTNT.com*

Opposite page
Top - Cocoa preparation
Bottom - Rice fields in Barrackpore, south Trinidad

J. BROWNE

F. KHAN

ANGOSTURA LIMITED

The history of the Angostura company began in Venezuela in 1824. Dr J.G.B. Siegert, a German-born surgeon in Simon Bolivar's army, had developed an elixir which proved effective against stomach and digestive disorders. This formula, which was made from various medicinal barks, herbs and spices, was named after the Venezuelan town of Angostura (now Ciudad Bolivar) on the Orinoco River.

The success of the 'aromatic bitters', which were also used to enhance the flavour of food and beverages, spread to many parts of the world, and a growing export market was established in nearby Trinidad and in England.

By the turn of the nineteenth century, the company had ventured into the rum market, and in 1949 erected a state-of-the-art distillery. By the end of the 1960s, Angostura Limited had extended the distribution of its products to over 140 countries, becoming well-known internationally for its high quality rums in addition to its world famous Angostura Bitters.

Angostura bitters, made by the Angostura brewing company, is a product synonymous with Trinidad and Tobago

Above right, down
Deep sea fishing vessel

Headquarters of the Oilfield Workers Trade Union (OWTU) on Circular Road in San Fernando. The union is one of the most powerful in the country

New housing at Trincity, two miles from Piarco Airport

Opposite page
Preparing clay for the potter

N. NORTON

MISONS INDUSTRIES

Misons Industries Ltd, left, is the most recent member of the Misons Group of Companies. The Group has its origins in the garment manufacturing sector where the group's founder, M.I. Juman, was one of the early pioneers of mass production in Trinidad.

The company's venture into the world of disposable diapers (nappies) in 1992 was a challenge, as this sector was already highly competitive. However, Misons was convinced that it could make a difference and has since revolutionised the local diaper industry with the introduction of sophisticated Italian state of the art machinery and equipment capable of high speed production.

The group's products - 'Teddies' and 'Cuties' disposable diapers, and 'Van Heusen' shirts, slacks and suits - can be found throughout the Caribbean as well as in Latin America.

With manufacturing plants in Trinidad and Barbados as well as a distributor/commission agency, property rentals, a shopping mall complex and holiday resorts, the group continues to grow and diversify its operations employing hundreds of nationals.

Calendar of festivals and public holidays

JANUARY
New Year's Day
1 January. Public Holiday

FEBRUARY
Carnival
Monday and Tuesday before Ash Wednesday
Shivratri
Hindu festival to honour Lord Shiva

MARCH
Phagwa
Also known as Holi, this Hindu festival heralds the arrival of Spring
Spiritual Baptist Liberation Day
30 March. Public Holiday. Honours the indigenous Shouter Baptist faith

APRIL
Good Friday
Public Holiday
Easter Monday
Public Holiday
Point Fortin Borough Week

MAY
La Divina Pastora
Roman Catholic festival held in Siparia on the second Sunday after Easter
Indian Arrival Day
30 May. Public Holiday. Marks the anniversary of the arrival of the first Indian indentured labourers in 1845

JUNE
Ganga Dashara
Hindu Festival of Rivers
Labour Day
19 June. Public Holiday
Corpus Christi
Sugar and Energy Festival
Held in Couva

JULY
Tobago Heritage Festival
Eid ul Fitr
Marks the end of Ramadan, the Muslim month of fasting. Actual dates are based on the Islamic calendar and may fall from June to August

AUGUST
Emancipation Day
1 August. Public Holiday. Celebrates the abolition of slavery in the British Caribbean colonies in 1834.
Santa Rosa Festival
Held in Arima to celebrate the nation's Amerindian history
Independence Day
31 August. Public Holiday

SEPTEMBER
Republic Day
24 September
Hosay
Festival to honour Muslim martyrs. Actual dates are based on the Islamic calendar and may fall from September to October

OCTOBER
Ramleela
Re-enactment of the Hindu epic, *The Ramayana*

NOVEMBER
Divali
Hindu Festival of Lights. Symbolises the triumph of light over dark. Actual dates are based on the phases of the moon and may fall within October or November
Kartik
Hindu ceremony of ritual cleansing which takes place at the sea shore

DECEMBER
Christmas Day
25 December. Public Holiday
Boxing Day
26 December. Public Holiday

Places of interest

Aripo Caves, St George
Aripo Savannah, St Andrew
Asa Wright Nature Centre, St George
Botanical Gardens, Queen's Park Savannah, Port of Spain
Caroni Arena Dam, San Rafael
Caroni Swamp, Caroni
Carrera Prison Island
Cathedral of The Holy Trinity, Queen Street, Port of Spain
Cathedral of the Immaculate Conception, Independence Square, Port of Spain
Chaguaramas Military History and Aviation Museum, Chaguaramas
Cumaca Caves, St Andrew
Emperor Valley Zoo, Queen's Park Savannah, Port of Spain
Fort George, St James
Galera Lighthouse, Galera Point, St David
Gasparee Caves, Gaspar Grande island
Hindu Mandir, 'Temple in the Sea', Waterloo, Caroni
Hollis Reservoir, Valencia
Jasmine's Ocean Resort nature centre, Balandra
La Vega Garden Centre, Caroni
Lighthouse, Chacachacare Island
Lopinot Complex, Arouca
Memorial Park, Frederick Street, Port of Spain
Mount St Benedict Monastery, St Augustine
Nariva Swamp, Nariva
National Museum, Frederick Street, Port of Spain
Navet Dam, Nariva
North Post, St George
Paradise Estate nature reserve, Aripo
Pitch Lake, La Brea
Point Lisas Industrial Estate, Couva
Pointe-a-Pierre Wild Fowl Trust, Victoria
President's House, Queen's Park Savannah, Port of Spain
Red House (Houses of Parliament), Abercromby Street, Port of Spain
River Estate Water Wheel, St George
Salt Pond, Chacachacare Island
San Fernando Hill, Victoria
The Devil's Wood Yard (mud volcanoes), Victoria
The Magnificent Seven, a row of lavish private houses built at the turn of the nineteenth century, Queen's Park Savannah, Port of Spain

BEACHES AND BAYS

Balandra, St Andrew
Blanchissuese, St George
Cedros, St Patrick
Cocos, Nariva
Columbus, St Patrick
Cumana, St David
Grande Riviere, St David
Grande Tacirib (access by boat/hiking), St George
Guayaguayare, Mayaro
Las Cuevas, St George
Los Iros, St Patrick
Macqueripe, Chaguaramas
Madamas (access by boat/hiking), St George
Manzanilla, St Andrew
Maracas, St George
Matura, St Andrew
Mayaro, Mayaro
Paria (access by boat/hiking), St George
Petit Tacirib (access by boat/hiking), St George
Quinam, St Patrick
Saline, St Andrew
Sans Souci, St David
Scotland Bay (access by boat), Chaguaramas
Toco, St David
Tyrico, St George

WATERFALLS

Blue Basin, St George
Edith Falls (only during height of rainy season), Tucker Valley, St George
Lalaja, St George
Madamas, Brasso Seco
Maracas, Maracas Valley, St Joseph
Petit Marianne, Marianne River, St George
Rincon, St George
Rio Seco/Salybia, St Andrew
Sombasson, St George

Sinopsis de Trinidad y Tobago

GEOGRAFIA

Trinidad y Tobago es una nación independiente que comprende las dos islas ubicadas en el extremo sur del archipiélago caribeño. Trinidad está situada a solo 7 millas de Venezuela. Tobago se encuentra 20 millas al norte de Trinidad. Trinidad es la más grande de las dos islas (1.864 millas cuadradas) y posee abundantes recursos naturales, en particular petróleo y gas natural que constituyen el eje de la economía de la nación. Fue parte del continente sudamericano en el pasado lo que le permite ostentar hoy en día una flora y fauna inexistente en las demás islas del Caribe. Su cordillera del norte es una estribación lejana de los Andes poderosos. Trinidad es un paraíso ecoturístico debido a su selva tropical rica, sus sabanas, manglares e inmensas extensiones de playas despobladas. Tobago es mucho más pequeña con una superficie que mide solamente 116 millas cuadradas, pero su belleza compensa para su tamaño: un interior montañoso de selva tropical que cae hacia playas idílicas cubiertas de arena blanca, rodeadas por barreras coralinas y aguas azules. Tobago representa el centro de la industria turistica del país. Ambas islas están ubicadas al sur de la zona de huracanes.

Port of Spain, la capital de la nación, se encuentra en el noroeste de Trinidad. Scarborough es la capital administrativa de Tobago. Port of Spain es una ciudad con mucha vida y movimiento, el eje comercial y financiero del país y la sede del gobierno. Quizás, ofrece la posibilidad de realizar las compras más interesantes en el Caribe, con sus tiendas elegantes y sus centros comerciales frescos y espaciosos que conviven junto a los mercados animados y bazares vivos. Port of Spain es la cuna del carnaval más sofisticado y magnífico del mundo.

UNA NACION ARCO IRIS

Trinidad y Tobago es uno de los países de mayor variedad cultural del mundo. La población de 1,3 millón proviene principalmente de los descendientes de esclavos africanos y de trabajadores contratados provenientes de las Indias Orientales después de la emancipación. Los chinos, sirios, libaneses y portugueses llegaron posteriormente. Colón descubrió la isla la cual estuvo bajo el dominio de los británicos, franceses y españoles por años, pero fueron los británicos los que mantuvieron el control de la isla, agregando a Tobago a la Corona de la Colonia en el año de 1888.

Trinidad es una amalgama cultural que se refleja en sus numerosos feriados nacionales. 'La Tierra de los Festivales', celebra el carnaval por supuesto, el Festival Tobago Heritage, Divali (el Festival de las Luces Hindú), Eid-ul-Fitr y Hosay de los musulmanes; hay también un día especial para los bautistas. Todo esto se refleja en su comida, moda, arquitectura, tradiciones y religiones. Los principales grupos religiosos son: católicos romanos, hindues y musulmanes. También son populares los bautistas espirituales, diversas iglesias evangelistas y algunos sistemas de creencias africanas como rasta, orisha y shango.

Existe una extraordinaria variedad de excelente gastronomía en Trinidad que representa a todas partes del mundo. La comida india tiene una gran influencia, ya sea que se trate de 'doubles' (garbanzos guisados con curry envueltos en una masa frita) que se come como un desayuno rápido, o 'roti' (curry envuelto en una masa blanda), quizás la más popular de toda la comida rápida local. Se puede degustar la influencia africana en los platos criollos tradicionales, mientras que la comida china es de excelente calidad y bien representada. En Port of Spain se encuentran muchos restaurantes elegantes que ofrecen comida oriental, italiana, francesa, polinesia, portuguesa, tailandesa e internacional.

CULTURA DEL CARNAVAL

El carnaval de Trinidad es el que inspira todos los carnavales del estilo caribeño, sea en Antigua, Nueva York o Notting Hill. No hay nada en el mundo que pueda preparar al visitante para la increíble explosión de color y música, y para los extraordinarios y extravagantes disfraces que hacen que el carnaval de Trinidad sea el más emocionante del mundo.

Oficialmente, se celebra el carnaval durante los dos días antes del miércoles de ceniza, pero de hecho, la temporada del carnaval empieza el primer día del nuevo año, lo que significa el inicio de dos meses cuando existe una contagiosa fiebre de carnaval en todo el país que está inundado de "fetes" (fiestas de carnaval), donde hay interpretaciones de las bandas más populares de la música soca. El carnaval penetra todo. Si hay una capital de fiesta en el mundo, es sin duda, Trinidad.

El carnaval y Trinidad y Tobago se caracterizan por la música. Calipso, soca (una versión más bailable del calipso) y steelpan conforman la banda sonora del carnaval y de la isla. Tanto el calipso como el steepan nacieron en Trinidad. El steelpan es el único instrumento musical no eléctrico inventado durante este siglo, un rasgo de genio que se atribuyó a Winston Spree Simon en los años treinta. Es el instrumento nacional del país. En el campeonato nacional "Panorama" durante el carnaval y en los eventos organizados a lo largo del año, se pueden ver las mejores orquestas de instrumentos de acero del mundo con más de 100 músicos en ciertas ocasiones. Las bandas como AMOCO Renegades y WITCO Desperadoes difunden el steelpan al resto del mundo mediante sus giras internacionales.

Peter Minshall es el diseñador más famoso de disfraces para el carnaval. Sus magníficos diseños fueron los que se presentaron durante las ceremonias inaugurales de los últimos dos Juegos Olímpicos.

La música es un elemento inseparable de la vida en T&T. El calipso es la más popular y representa un permiso para criticar a los polÍticos y a cualquier otra persona por medio del uso de rimas ingeniosas y rítmos vivos. Los diversos grupos étnicos han asimilado la música de los demás grupos y la han fusionado: 'chutney-soca', una mezcla de los sonidos indios con el rítmo de soca; 'reggae-soca', soca mezclada con dancehall reggae; 'rapso', una combinación de rítmos africanos y soca; 'parang' es la música navideña de T&T, que tiene su origen en los villancicos venezolanos, cantada en español con un acompañamiento acústico muy pegajoso.

ECONOMIA Y COMERCIO

Se ha dicho que Trinidad y Tobago es 'la gran historia de éxito en el Caribe', 'un tigre económico en un mar de gatos'. Estas descripciones son muy apropiadas ya que T&T se encuentra en los primeros lugares de inversión en el Caribe, con el nivel per cápita más alto de inversión extranjera directa de cualquier país en el hemisferio occidental, con la excepción de Canada. La posición de Trinidad como la capital comercial del Caribe se fortalece mediante los bajos costos de energía, por una fuerza laboral bien calificada y formada, por la infraestructura y telecomunicaciones modernas junto a un estable sistema político democrático.

La mayoría de la inversión interna se ha dirigido al sector de energía que representa casi 72% de las exportaciones del país. Las reservas considerables de energía (petróleo, 0,84 mil millones be barriles; gas natural, 25,3 billones de pies cúbicos en franco aumento) han permitido que el país se convierta en el más industrializado del Caribe; es el exportador más grande de amoniaco y el productor principal de asfalto, metanol, urea y acero. El centro industrial y de energía de T&T es Point Lisas, donde está ubicada la fábrica más grande de gas natural líquido en la historia de la región.

A pesar de la dependencia de la energía y debido a los precios petroleros cambiantes, los gobiernos sucesivos han sido obligados a diversificar la economía de Trinidad y Tobago hacia otras áreas. Estas áreas incluyen la expansión del sector industrial y el sector agrícola, como, por ejemplo, el procesamiento de alimentos, la transformación de madera, embalaje, productos farmacéuticos, la industria textil, servicios marítimos y las industrias de construcción. Entre los sectores de mayor crecimiento en la actualidad, figuran la informática, los servicios financieros, el turismo y hospedaje, los servicios ambientales, el entretenimiento y la diversión.

En términos estratégicos, T&T no puede tener una mejor ubicación. Se encuentra en la encrucijada comercial de las Américas, una posición perfecta para aprovechar los inmensos mercados que se abren entre Sudamérica, América Central y Norteamérica y el Caribe. T&T es signatario de una serie de tratados comerciales progresivos con los Estados Unidos, Canada, el Reino Unido, Francia, Brasil, Argentina, España, el Mercado Común de Centroamérica (MCCA), la Comunidad Caribeña (CARICOM) y la Unión Europea (LOME IV).

TIDCO - Tourism and Industrial Development Company of Trinidad and Tobago (la Compañía de Turismo y Desarrollo Industrial de Trinidad y Tobago), es la agencia gubernamental responsable del desarrollo económico que comercializa en el exterior, la economía de Trinidad y Tobago impulsado por los mercados, sus atractivos paquetes de inversión, y su atracción como una isla doble que constituye un paraíso turístico. HYPERLINK http://www.tidco.co.tt. El sector turístico genera la mayoría de los ingresos de Tobago. Es una de las islas mejor conservadas y más hermosas del Caribe, dado que su encanto y caracter no han sido afectados por el turismo en masa. En su lugar, por muchos años, Tobago ha establecido como su meta, el mercado de vacaciones más perspicaz, con el resultado de que en gran parte, el desarrollo ha dependido de estructuras de afición, edificios no elevados y atractivos, mezclados con el entorno circundante. En el año 2000, se pondrá en marcha el proyecto turístico más grande en la historia de Trinidad y Tobago, el centro Tobago Plantations de cinco estrellas y Tobago Hilton en Lowlands. El eje turístico de la isla está situado en la region del suroeste, en las proximidades de Crown Point y su aeropuerto internacional. El turismo se desarrolla rápidamente en Trinidad, siempre bajo el enfoque del ecoturismo y los eventos relacionados con los festivales como el carnaval. El Acta de Hoteles y Desarrollo de Trinidad y Tobago fomenta la entrada internacional en este mercado por medio de numerosos incentivos para atraer la inversión.

UNA HISTORIA NATURAL UNICA

Trinidad ofrece a los amantes de la naturaleza la oportunidad de experimentar la selva tropical de Sudamérica sin necesidad de pisar el continente. Cuando Trinidad se separó del continente, un gran porcetaje de sus habitantes primitivos y vegetación original vino con la isla. Esta proximidad ha dado a las islas, una historia muy distinta del resto del Caribe. Trinidad tiene una flora y fauna típica de la cadena caribeña además de la selva tropical del continente.

En Trinidad hay 433 especies de pájaros y 250 de estas especies se reproducen en al isla. 'La Tierra del Colibrí' tiene 41 especies brillantes de esas pequeñas maravillas aladas. El centro de naturaleza Asa Wright (Asa Wright Nature Centre) ubicado en la cordillera del norte, es una de las áreas más extraordinarias de todo el mundo para observar pájaros. En Tobago hay 13 especies de pájaros adicionales que no se encuentran en Trinidad.

La Fauna de Trinidad

622 especies de mariposas, 108 mamíferos que incluyen el mono aullador rojo, ocelote, manatí, armadillo, pecarí, puerco espín arborícolo, ciervo y laudes gigantes que vienen a la costa del norte de Trinidad y a Tobago para poner sus huevos. 70 clases de reptiles, 57 especies de murciélagos, 2300 matorrales y plantas florecientes, 700 especies de orquídeas.

SITIOS DE INTERES Y ACTIVIDADES

TRINIDAD

Queen's Park Savannah - una sabana donde el visitante se puede relajar con sus amigos, pasearse, comer maíz en la mazorca o ostras, jugar cricket o rugby o asistir a un fesitval de música. Además, es el punto culminante del carnaval. Ofrece también las 'Magnificent Seven': siete casas coloniales ubicadas en el perímetro occidental empleadas hoy en día para distintos propósitos

Los Jardines Botánicos (Botanical Gardens)

El campo de cricket Queen's Park Oval, el campo natal de Brian Lara

Red House (la Casa Roja), el gran edificio del Parlamento situado en Woodford Square

Brian Lara Promenade, el sitio de relajamiento en el centro de la ciudad de Port of Spain

La Calle Frederick y sus alrededores para hacer compras

Chaguaramas – ubicado en la península al noroeste de la isla, que fue la sede del concurso de Miss Universo 1999

Chaguaramas National Park – valles bellísimos poblados de árboles y repletos de fauna. Se ofrecen visitas organizadas por la CDA

Marinas, navegación y pesca – Chaguaramas está situada fuera de la zona de huracanes y constituye el centro de la industria de servicios marítimos. Ofrece modernas marinas, restaurantes, clubes y tiendas que han sido diseñados con elegancia, y que se encuentran a todo lo largo de esta costa hermosa

La playa Maqueripe y Scotland Bay

Chaguaramas Public Golf Course: un desafiante campo de golfo público, de nueve hoyos en medio de un escenario bello

'Down the islands': islas ubicadas fuera de Chaguaramas, solitarias y tranquilas, un destino muy popular para los fines de semana

MARAVILLAS NATURALES

La costa del norte y la cordillera del norte – un área que posee una belleza extraordinaria con magníficas playas, que ofrece al visitante una oportunidad excelente para ir de excursión y observar los pájaros. Se puede obtener de TIDCO, una lista de los operadores de eco-visitas, hoteles y posadas

El Tucuche – el segundo pico más alto de la isla (936m), una escalada exigente que vale la pena

El premiado Asa Wright Nature Centre es la reserva situada en la cordillera del norte que ofrece excursiones, alojamiento y un centro de estudios

Aripo Caves – un conjunto inmenso de cuevas, cuna del guácharo ciego

Caroni Swamp – un misterioso manglar ubicado una media hora de Port of Spain; cuna del colorido Ibis Escarleta, el pájaro nacional del país

Nariva Swamp – un área excepcional de interés científco, situada cerca de la playa Manzanilla en el este; cuna de monos, anacondas y manatíes

Las playas Grande Riviere, Matelot, Matura y Rincorn – áreas visitadas por los laudes gigantes que vienen para poner sus huevos

Pointe-a-Pierre Wild Fowl Trust – una reserva ubicada en los jardines de una refinería de petróleo

Pitch Lake - Un lago de brea que se revuelve de una manera imperceptible sobre el que se puede andar. Sir Walter Raleigh utilizó la sustancia para calafatear sus barcos. Se exporta esta brea de alta calidad y se la utiliza para pavimentar las calles desde Londres hasta Nueva York

Devi's Woodyard – una misteriosa área geológica en la que se pueden observar volcanes de lodo en miniatura

Playas - Maracas, Las Cuevas, Blanchisseuse, Paria, Matelot, Grande Riviere y Toco, todas playas idílicas ubicadas en la costa del norte. En la costa del este, se puede disfrutar de Balandra Bay y de las playas Manzanilla y Mayaro, donde una extensión infinita de cocoteros se enfrenta al Atlántico salvaje. Además, hay playas en el península Cedros en el suroueste de la isla

OTRAS ATRACCIONES

Mt. St. Benedict Monastery– el monasterio benedictino más antiguo en el Caribe, con una vista espectacular de las llanuras del centro de Trinidad

Angostura Distillery – extraordinarias visitas para observar la fabricación del ron y del mundialmente famoso Angostura Bitters

Waterloo Temple – un templo hindú construido en el mar

San Fernando – la segunda ciudad de Trinidad

DEPORTES
Cricket - Queen's Park Oval, o en cualquier espacio abierto.
Golf - St. Andrew's, Moka, cerca de Port of Spain; Chaguaramas Public Course de nueve hoyos; Pointe-a-Pierre Golf Club, cerca de Point Lisas.
Fútbol - Hasely Crawford National Stadium, Centre of Excellence.
Atletismo - Hasely Crawford National Stadium.
Tenis - Jean Pierre Complex.
Navegación y pesca - Chaguaramas y la costa del norte.

TOBAGO
Buceo y buceo con esnórquel – Tobago ofrece las experiencias de buceo más increíbles del Caribe. Entre las zonas extraordinarias figuran: Speyside, donde se puede nadar junto a las mantas y también Charlotteville y Giles Islands ubicadas en el norte de la isla; Buccoo Reef y la mayoría de la costa de sotavento, en particular Mt. Irvine, Arnos Vale, Culloden Bay y Castara

Eco-Tobago – Northern Forest Reserve, la reserva forestal más antigua del hemisferio occidental; Little Tobago y Arnos Vale son excelentes sitios para observar los pájaros; Turtle Beach donde se puede observar a los laudes que vienen para poner sus huevos; Argyll Falls

Playas – hay una extraordinaria cantidad de playas hermosas en Tobago. Las mejores son: Pigeon Point y Store Bay situadas cerca de Crown Point; Mt. Irvine Bay y Courland Bay un poco más al norte, Castara, Englishmsn's Bay y Bloody Bay ubicadas más arriba en la costa de sotavento; en la costa de barlovento se puede disfrutar Bacolet Bay, Fort Granby, Kings Bay y Speyside famosa por su tranquilidad

Deportes acuativos - se puede encontrar lo mejor en Pigeon Point donde la laguna es perfecta para hacer esquí aquático y windsurfing

Pesca – hay una abundancia de peces cazados como recreo en las aguas de Tobago. Carib Beer International Game Fishing Tournament es un concurso internacional muy esperado, que se celebra cada año durante la Pascua

Golf - el campo de golf en Mt. Irvine Bay para competencias internacionales, el campo diseñado por Jack Nicklaus para campeonatos en Tobago Plantations en Lowlands

Carreras de cabras y cangrejos – en Buccoo, la sede de las carreras de cabras y cangrejos del mundo; una oportunidad de presenciar diferentes carreras cada fin de semana Santa

Scarborough – Fort King George, ubicado en una colina rodeado de atractivos paisajes, con una vista completa de la costa y la capital; el museo de Tobago, en Barrack Guard House de Fort King George (un cuerpo de guardia), cuenta la historia sangrienta de la isla; los Jardines Botánicos

Trinidad et Tobago en bref

GEOGRAPHIE

Trinidad et Tobago est un pays indépendant qui consiste aux deux îles les plus au sud de l'archipel de la Caraïbe. Trinidad est situé à une distance de 11 km. de la côte du Vénézuela et Tobago à 35 km. au nord de Trinidad.

Trinidad, la plus grande des deux, a une superficie de 7,500 km.2 et des énormes réserves de ressources naturelles, particulièrement le pétrole et le gaz naturel qui représentent les industries les plus importantes du pays. Physiquement rattaché, dans un passé lointain, au continent de l'Amérique du Sud, Trinidad dispose d'une diversité de flore et faune incomparable pour une île caribéene. Au nord du pays, la chaîne de montagnes n'est qu'un pic distant des Andes majestueuses. Avec ses luxuriantes forêts tropicales, ses savanes, ses mangroves et ses vastes étendues de plages désertes, Trinidad est le paradis de l'éco-touriste.

Tobago, la petite sæur, a une superficie de 450 km.2. Pourtant, sa petite taille est recompensée par la beauté de son intérieur montagneux et boisé, et par ses formidables plages tranquilles de sable blanc entourées des récifs de corail et sa mer d'azur. Tobago est le centre de l'industrie touristique du pays.

Les deux îles se situent au sud du parcours habituel des cyclones tropicaux.

La capitale de Trinidad et Tobago est la ville de Port of Spain, située au nord-ouest de Trinidad, tandis que Scarborough est la capitale administrative de Tobago. Port of Spain, une ville dynamique et énergique, est le centre de la vie commerciale du pays aussi bien que le siège du gouvernement. Avec ses magasins chic, ses grands centres commerciaux, élégants, spacieux et côte à côte avec des marchés pittoresques et des boutiques animés, Port of Spain offre une activité commerciale qui est unique dans la Caraïbe. En plus, c'est ici que se trouve le Carnaval le plus extravagant et le plus spectaculaire du monde.

PAYS ARC-EN-CIEL

Trinidad et Tobago est un des pays les plus multi-culturels du monde. La population, 1.3 million, consiste principalement de descendants d'esclaves africains, et d'ouvriers indiens venus après l'abolition de l'esclavage. Pendant les années suivantes, les Chinois, les Syriens, les

Libanais et les Portugais ont ajouté leur présence. Découvert par Christophe Colomb, Trinidad a été soumis à la domination anglaise, française et espagnole aux différentes périodes, mais ce sont finalement les Anglais qui l'ont emporté, annexant en 1888 l'île de Tobago pour former la colonie.

Le mélange de cultures qui est Trinidad se manifeste dans ses nombreux festivals. Voici le pays de festivals! Tout d'abord, il y a le Carnaval, bien sûr, puis le Festival d'Héritage de Tobago, le Divali – le Festival Hindou de Lumières, les Festivals musulmans – Eid-Ul-Fitr et Hosay; et même un jour pour les Baptistes. Toutes cettes diversités éthniques et évidentes dans la cuisine, les modes, l'architecture, les traditions et les religions.

Les religions les plus importantes sont le Catholicisme, l'Hinduisme et l'Islam. Les Baptistes aussi, sont nombreux et il y a plusieurs églises pentecôtes et croyances de base africaine tel que le Rastafari, l'Orisa et le Shango.

A Trinidad on peut trouver une somptueuse variété de cuisine de première classe, originaire de plusieurs pays. L'influence indienne est considerable; il y a les doubles – des poichiches au curry enveloppés dans deux pâtes et mangées à courir le matin. Il y a aussi le plus populaire des fast foods locaux – le roti: une pâte fourrée de pois-cassés jaunes. L'influence africaine se manifeste dans la cuisine créole, et la superbe cuisine chinoise se trouve partout. Les nombreux restaurants de classe qui se trouve dans la capital disposent d'une variété de cuisine de style arabe, italien, français, polynésien, portugais, thaïlandais et international.

LA CULTURE CARNAVAL

Le Carnaval de Trinidad est la source et l'inspiration de tous les carnavals de style caribéen soit celui de l'Antigue, celui de New York ou celui de Notting Hill. Il n'y a rien du monde qui se compare à l'explosion spectaculaire de couleurs et de musique et aux costumes extravagants qui destinguent le Carnaval de Trinidad comme le plus passionnant du monde.

Le Carnaval a lieu les deux jours qui précèdent le Mercredi de Cendres. Mais en réalité, la saison de Carnaval se lance le Jour de l'An, le début de deux mois fièvreux de célébrations infectueuses où toute l'île s'éclate en soirée de Carnaval, menées par le son palpitant des groupes de soca. A Trinidad, le Carnaval est omniprésent. S'il existe une capitale de fêtes du monde, c'est Trinidad.

Le Carnaval et Trinidad et Tobago lui-même trouvent leur inspiration dans la musique. Le calypso, le soca – une version de calypso faite pour danser – et le steel-band sont la musique typique du pays. Les deux sont originaires de Trinidad. Le steel-band, instrument national du pays, est la seule invention musicale non-electonique de ce siècle – un coup de génie attribué à Winston Spree Simon pendant les années trentes, Pendant toutes l'année et surtout pendant la période du Carnaval, lors de la grande compétition de steel-band – Panorama – on voit les meilleures orchestres du monde, certains consistant de plus de cent joueurs. Des groupes comme Amoco Renegades et Witco Desperadoes font la tour du monde, exposant la musique steel-band à une audience plus globale.

Le plus grand créateur de costumes de Carnaval, Peter Minshall, a contribué son talent étonnant à la conception des cérémonies d'ouverture de deux derniers Jeux Olympiques.

La musique et ton aspect inévitable de la vie à Trinidad et Tobago. La forme la plus populaire – le Calypso – représent un permis de fustiger en chanson piquante n'importe quel politicien ou individu. En adoptant les genres de l'un et l'autre, les divers groupes éthniques du pays ont crées une fusion musicale. Il y a le chutney-soca, un mélange de musique indienne et du soca, le ragga-soca – une combination du soca et le reggae, et le rapso – une fusion des rythmes africains et le soca. Et enfin, il y a le parang – la musique de Noël de Trinidad et Tobago, une dérivation de cantiques vénézuéléenes, chantées en espagnol et accompagnées d'une acoustique contagieuses.

ECONOMIE ET COMMERCE

Trinidad et Tobago mérite bien sa réputation du "Grand succès de la Caraïbe" et du "Tigre économique parmi des chatons." A l'exception du Canada, dans aucun pays de l'hémisphère n'y a-t-il un niveau d'investissement direct per habitant aussi impressionnant. Les prix d'énergie bas, une main d'œuvre bien qualifiée, un système de télécommunications et infrastructure moderne, et un système politique qui est démocratique et stable, tous ces facteurs ont consolidé la position de Trinidad et Tobago de capital commerciale de la Caraïbe.

La pluspart de l'investissement est concentrée dans le secteur d'énergie qui compte pour 72% des exportations. Grace à ses importantes réserves d'énergies (le pétrole, 0.84 billons de barils; le gaz naturel, 774 billions de mètres cubes et en constante augmentation), Trinidad et Tobago a pu devenir le pays le plus industrialisé de la Caraïbe. C'est le plus grand exportateur d'ammoniac au monde et un exportateur principal d'asphalte, de méthanol, d'urée et d'acier. Le cœur du secteur d'énergie se trouve à Point Lisas, qui est également le site de la plus immense plante de gaz naturel liquéfié de toute la région.

Après une longe dépendance de cette industrie d'énergie, les fluctuations des prix internationaux du pétrole ont forcé les gouvernements du pays de diversifié l'économie vers d'autres secteurs tel que la fabrication, l'agriculture, l'agro-alimentaires, l'industrie de bois et l'industrie d'emballage, les pharmaceutiques, le textile, les services maritimes, et la construction. Il y a aussi, les secteurs émergents tel que l'informatique, les services de finance, le tourisme, l'environnment, le spectacle et le loisir.

Au niveau strategique, Trinidad est parfaitement situé dans la croisée de commerce entre les Amériques, et donc, idéalment placé pour profité des vastes marchés émergents en Amérique Latine, Amérique du Nord et la Caraïbe. Le pays fait partie de plusieurs accords commerciaux avec les Etats-Unis, le Canada, la Grande Bretagne, la France, le Brésil, l'Argentine, l'Espagne, le Marché Commun de l'Amérique Centrale, le CARICOM et l'Europe.

La compétitivité de l'economie de Trinidad et Tobago, l'attrait de ses favorables conditions pour l'investissements et son image séduisant d'île-jumelles paradis, voici les atouts à la base des efforts acharnés du gouvernement de ce pays pour vendre Trinidad et Tobago à l'étranger, à travers son agence chargée du développement économique – Tourism and Industrial Development Company of

Trinidad and Tobago (TIDCO). HYPERLINK http://www.tidco.co.tt. Le tourisme est l'industrie la plus importante de Tobago, une des ïles les plus vierges et les plus belles de la Caraïbes, son charme et son caractère peu touchés par le tourisme de masse. Tobago a toujours ciblé le marché 'loisir' et par conséquent, son développement est caracterisé par des discrètes structures de goût, construites avec modération et attirantes, co-existant en harmonie avec les environs naturels. En 2000, Trinidad et Tobago lancera son plus grand projet touristique, les stations banléaires 5-étoiles Tobago Plantations et l'Hilton Tobago à Lowlands. L'activité touristique est concentrée au sud-ouest aux environs de Crown Point et son aéroport international.

Le secteur touristique de Trinidad est en pleine expansion, le tourisme-vert et les festivals étant les aspects les plus mis en valeur. L'Acte d'Hôtellerie et Développement de Trinidad et Tobago encourage l'investissement étranger dans ce secteur.

EXCEPTIONNEL HERITAGE NATUREL

Pour l'enthousiaste de la nature, Trinidad offre l'expérience des forêts tropicales de l'Amérique du Sud sans devoir y aller. Au cours du détachement géographique du continent, un grand nombre d'espèces animales et végétales s'est laissé à Trinidad. C'est cette proximité qui rend à ces îles-jumelles un caractère géographique bien différent du reste de la Caraïbe – une diversité de flore et faune typique des îles caribéenes et forêts continentales en même temps.

Il y a 433 espèces d'oiseaux à Trinidad, dont 250 se reproduisent sur l'île. Dans cette Terre du Colibri se trouvent 41 espèces brillantes de cette merveille. Le Centre Asa Wright, au nord, est un des meilleurs du monde pour l'observation d'oiseaux. A Tobago il y a 13 espèces d'oiseaux qui ne se trouvent pas à Trinidad.

La Faune de Trinidad

622 espèces de papillon, 108 mammifères tel que le macaque rouge, l'ocelot, le lamentin, l'armadillo, le sanglier, le porc-épic des arbres, et la biche. Les tortues marines "leatherback" se nichent le long de la côte nord de Trinidad aussi bien qu'à Tobago. 70 espèces reptiliennes, 57 espèces de chauve-souris, 2,200 variétés de plantes et fleurs, 700 variétés d'orchidées.

A VISITER ET A FAIRE

TRINIDAD

La Savane 'Queen's Park' – pour flâner, faire des promenades, manger des huîtres du maïs bouilli, des partis de cricket ou de rugby, des festivals de musique et des grands specacles de Carnaval. Au périmètre à l'Est de la Savane, 'les Magnifique Sept' des grandes démeures coloniales qui se servent aujourd'hui de diverses fonctions

Les Jardins Botaniques

Le Stade de cricket 'Queen's Park Oval' - l'arène de Brian Lara

La Maison Rouge- le grand siège de parlement à la Place Woodford

La Promenade Brian Lara – lieu de réunion des flâneurs de Port of Spain

La rue Frederick et ses environs, pour les achats

Chaguaramas – à la péninsule nord-ouest de l'île, ville-hôtesse du Concours Miss Universe 1999

Chaguaramas National Park – des belles vallées boisées et abondantes en faune. Des tours guidés arrangés par le Chaguaramas Development Authority

Marinas, voile, pêche – hors du parcours des cyclones, Chaguaramas est le centre de l'industrie marine

Tout au long de cette merveilleuse étendue de côte, on voit des marinas modernes, des restaurants, des clubs et des magasins – tous conçus avec goût

La Plage Macqueripe et Scotland Bay

Chaguaramas Public Golf Course: terrain de golf exigeant dans un joli milieu

Le tour des Ilots – les îlots 'Bocas' près de Chaguaramas, déserts, tranquils, lieu d'évasion populaire pour passer le week-end

MERVEILLES NATURELLES

La Côte Nord et la Chaîne du Nord – un lieu de beauté exceptionnelle et de magnifiques plages, offrant des marches fascinantes et une excellente observation d'oiseaux. Des renseignements sur les tours-opérateurs, les hôtels, et les auberges sont disponibles aux bureaux de TIDCO

El Tucuche – deuxième pic (936 m) de l'île, une montée épuisante mais satisfaisante

Asa Wright Nature Centre – gagnant des prix pour sa beauté exceptionelle, cette réserve naturelle située dans le Nord offre des tours guidés, du logement, et une bibliothèque.
Les Grottes d'Aripo – grand complexe de grottes et l'habitat du 'Oilbird aveugle'

Caroni Swamp - mangrove mystérieuse située à une demie-heure de Port of Spain, l'habitat de l'oiseau national (l'Ibis Rouge)

Nariva Swamp – mangrove située près de la plage Manzanilla à l'Est du pays, Nariva est un lieu de grand intérêt scientifique, et l'habitat de singes, anacondas et lamentins

Les plages de Grande Rivière, Matelot, Matura et Rincon – lieux de niche de la Tortue Marine 'Leatherback'

Pointe-à-Pierre Wild Fowl Trust – réserve d'oiseaux située sur le terrain d'une raffinerie pétrolière

Le Pitch Lake – un lac d'asphalte bouillonnant, mais assez ferme pour permettre les tours à pied. C'est ici que Sir Walter Raleigh a pu calfater ses navires. Cette asphalte haute qualité est exportée partout dans le monde, et serve de paver les rues de Londres jusqu'à celles de New York

Le 'Devil's Woodyard' - bizarre lieu géologique de volcans de boue miniatures

Plages - Maracas, Las Cuevas, Blanchisseuse, Paria, Matelot, Grande Rivière, et Toco sur la Côte Nord, toutes désertes. Sur la Côte Est, il y a les plages Balandra, Manzanilla et Mayaro où des bandes interminables de cocotiers font face à l'Atlantique sauvage. Des plages se trouvent également à la péninsule de Cedros au Sud-Ouest

AUTRES ATTRACTIONS

Le Monastère de Mont St. Bénédicte – offrant une vue spectaculaire des plaines centrales, Mt. St. Bénédicte est le plus ancien des monastères bénédictins de la région

La Distillerie Angostura – présentation impressionnante du monde de rhum et du célèbre 'Angostura Bitters'

Le Temple Waterloo – temple hindou construit dans la mer par un seul homme

San Fernando - la deuxième ville de Trinidad

SPORTS
Cricket - joué au Stade 'Queen's Park', ou à n'importe quel espace ouvert

Golf - les terrains principaux près de Port of Spain sont St. Andrews et Moka. Il y a aussi le Terrain Public 9-trous à Chaguaramas, le Club de Golf à Pointe-à-Pierre, près de Point Lisas

Football - le Stade National Hasely Crawford et le Centre d' Excellence

Athlétisme - le Stade National Hasely Crawford

Tennis - le Jean Pierre Complex

Voile et Pêche - Chaguaramas et la Côte Nord

TOBAGO
La plongée et le snorkeling - les eaux de Tobago offrent la plongée la plus sensationnelle de la Caraïbe

Les meilleurs lieux de plongée sont: Speyside, où l'on peut nager avec des raies Manta, Charlotteville et les Ilots Giles au nord du pays. Il y aussi. Buccoo Reef et la plupart de la Côte Leeward, surtout à Mount Irvine, Arnos Vale, Culloden Bay et Castara

Eco-Tobago - le Northern Forest Reserve, la plus ancienne réserve naturelle de l'hémisphère ouest, Little Tobago et Arnos Vale pour les observateurs d'oiseaux, Turtle Beach pour ceux qui s'intéressent a la Tortue Marine 'Leatherback', et enfin, Argyll Falls

Plages - des belles plages abondent à Tobago, dont les meilleurs sont: Pigeon Point et Store Bay, près de l'aéroport de Crown Point; Mt. Irvine Bay et Courland Bay un peu plus vers le nord; Castara, Englishman's Bay et Bloody Bay plus loin sur la Côte Leeward. Sur la Côte Windward où la mer est généralement moins calme, il y a les plages de Lowlands, Bacolet Bay, Fort Granby, King's Bay, et Speyside où la mer est assez calme

Sport Nautique - La lagune de Pigeon Point offre les meilleures conditions pour la planche à voile et le ski nautique

Pêche - Les eaux de Tobago sont abondantes en poissons de sport

Chaque année, à Pâques, on y voit le grand évènement sportif – le Grand Tournoi de Pêche , sponsorisé par la brasserie 'Carib Beer'

Golf - Le terrain de Mt. Irvine, tout neuf et conceptualisé par Jack Nicklaus, ce terrain fait partie de Tobago Plantations à Lowlands.
Courses de crabes et de chèvres - Courses régulières à Buccoo, la capitale de ce sport passionnant et imprévisible

Scarborough - Fort King George, perché sur un morne dans un beau terrain, et donnant un panorama Formidable de la côte et la capitale. Le musée de Tobago,situé au Caserne à Fort King George, raconte l'histoire sanglante de l'île

Trinidad und Tobago Eine Übersicht

GEOGRAPHISCH

Trinidad and Tobago ist ein unabhängiger Staat, der aus zwei Inseln besteht die südlichsten der Karibik. Trinidad liegt gerade sieben Meilen (ungefähr 12 km) vor der Küste Venezulas. Tobago liegt 20 Meilen (ungefähr 35 km) nördlich vor Trinidad.

Trinidad ist die grössere der beiden Inseln mit ungefähr 1864 Square Meilen (ungefähr 7500qkm) und ist reich an Bodenschätzen, insbesondere Erdöl und Erdgas, die auch das Rückrat der staatlichen Wirtschaft sind. Es wird angenommen, dass Trinidad einst Teil des südamerikanischen Festlandes war. Daher auch die für die Karibik ungewöhnliche, einzigartige und mannigfaltige Flora und Fauna. Der nördliche Bergzug ist ein entfernter Ausläufer der mächtigen Anden. Reich an Regenwäldern, Savannahs, Sümpfen und langestreckten, einsamen, idyllischen Stränden, ist Trinidad ein Paradies des Öko-Tourismus.

Tobago ist wesentlich kleiner mit nur 116 Square Meilen (ungefähr 450qkm). Was es an Fläche mangelt macht es wett an Schönheit: hügelige Regenwälder im Landesinnern, die bis auf die weissandigen idyllischen Strände hinunterpurzeln, umgeben bei Korallenriff und azurblauem Meer. Tobago ist das Zentrum des Tourismus von Trinidad und Tobago.

LAND DES REGENBOGENS

Trinidad und Tobago ist eins der multi-kulturellsten Länder der Erde. Die Bevölkerung beträgt 1,3 Millionen. Sie besteht in der Mehrzahl aus Nachkommen afrikanischer Sklaven und indischer Vertragsarbeiter, die nach der Slavenbefreiung nach Trinidad kamen. Späterhin wanderten auch Chinesen, Syrier, Lebanesen und Portugiesen zu. Briten, Franzosen und Spanier haben alle zu einer Zeit über die Insel geherrscht. Es waren aber die Briten, die Trinidad behielten und 1888 Tobago in die Kronkolonie miteinbezogen.

Der kulturelle Schmeltopf, den Trinidad behaust, spiegelt sich in den vielen Feiertagen wieder. "Das Land der Festlichkeiten".

Der Karnival, natürlich, in Tobago Fest in Erinnerung an Traditionen der Vorfahren, Heritage Festival genannt. Divali, das Fest der Lichter der Hindus und die muslimischen Feste Eid-ul-Fitr und Hosay. Es gibt sogar einen Feiertag für die Baptisten. All diese Traditionen spiegeln sich im Essen, der Kleidung, der

Architektur, der Gebräuche und Religionen wieder.

Die Hauptreligionen, die hier vertreten sind, sind Katholiken, Hindus und Muslims. Man findet auch eine beachtliche Vertretung von Spirituellen Baptisten, sowohl als auch einige Penetecostal Gruppen und Anhänger afrikanischer Glaubensgruppen wie Rastafari, Orisha und Shango.

Es gibt eine pikante Auswahl von erstklassigem Essen in Trinidad, das aus aller Welt kommt. Indische Küche ist von grossem Einfluss, ob es nun 'Doubles' sind (gemacht aus Kichererben mit Curry, eingewickelt in 'bara' [zwei kleine weiche in Öl gebackene Fladen]), die man zum Früstück auf die Schnelle isst, oder aber 'Roti' (Curry gewürztes Fleisch und/oder Gemüse eingewikelt in einen grossen weichen Fladen), das wohl das populärster aller Gerichte ist. Die afrikanische Küche kann man in den Kreole Gerichten geniessen (meistens kleingeschnittenes Fleisch mit stark gewürzter Sosse, oder auch Fisch, mit lokalem Gemüse und verschiedenen Kartoffelarten). Die chinesische Küche ist ganz besonders gut und sehr beliebt. Port of Spain hat viele ausgezeichnete Restaurants, die mittelöstliche, italienische, französische, polynesische, thailändische und andere internationale Küche anbieten.

KARNIVAL - EINE KULTUR

Der Trinidad Karnival ist der Karnival von dem alle karibik-artigen Karnivals ihre Inspiration herholen, ob es nun die Insel Antigua ist, New York oder Notting Hill in England. Nichts in der Welt kann den Besucher auf die atemberaubende Explosion von Farbe, Musik und aussergewöhnlichsten Kostümen vortbereiten, die Trinidad Karnival zum Spektalulärsten und Aufregendsten der Welt machen.

Offiziell findet der Karnival an den zwei Tagen vor Aschermittwoch statt. In Wirklichkeit fängt die Karnivalsaison aber schon direkt nach Silvester an. Zwei Monate lang voller ansteckendem Karnivalfieber. Die Insel ist überschwemmt mit Karnival Fêten, auf denen die schmissigsten Soca Bands spielen. Karnival durchdringt alle Fasern des Lebens. Wenn es überhaupt ein Party Zentrum der Welt gäbe, dann ist es sicherlich Trinidad.

Music ist die Triebkraft des Karnival und von Trinidad and Tobago. Calypso, Soca (eine Calypso version zum tanzen) und die Steelpan sind die Musik des Karnivals und der beiden Inseln. Calypso sowohl als auch Steelpan wurden in Trinidad 'geboren'. Die Steelpan ist das einzige nicht-elektronische Musikinstrument, das in diesem Jahrhundert erfunden wurde. Ein Geniestreich, welcher Winston Spree Simon zugeschrieben wird um 1930. Es ist das Nationalinstrument dieses Landes. Die feinsten Steel Orchester der Welt, mit manchmal über 100 Spielern, kann man hier sehen und hören zu den Panorama Championships, die besonders während der Karnivalzeit stattfinden, aber auch das Jahr über. Einige der Orchester wie AMOCO Renegades und WITCO Desperados gehen auf internationalen Touren und machen die Welt mit Steelpan bekannt.

Trinidad's berühmtester Kostümerzeichner und Karnival Gruppenführer ist Peter Minshall. Seine erstaunlichen Kreationen wurden sogar in den letzten zwei Olympischen Spielen während der Eröffnungsfeiern aufgeführt.

Die Musik ist ein unentrinnbarer Teil des trinidadischen und tobagonischen Lebens. Davon ist Calypso die populärste Musikform; mit geistreichen Reimen und schmissiger Melodie, eine Lizenz die Politiker 'herunterzuputzen' oder auch jeden anderen. Die diversen ethnischen Gruppen haben ihre Musik miteinander verbunden und verschmolzen, so zum Beispiel ist 'Chutney-Soca' eine Mischung von indischer Musik und Soca Rythmen; 'Ragga-Soca' eine Mischung von Soca und Reggae Tanzmusik; 'Rapso' verschmilzt afrikanisch-basierte Musik mit Soca; 'Parang' wiederun ist Trinidad und Tobago's Weihnachtsmusik, die ihren Ursprung in venezuelanischen Weihnachtsliedern hat und daher in spanisch gesungen wird, begleitet von unwiderstehlich akustischer Untermalung.

WIRTSCHAFT UND INDUSTRIE

Trinidad und Tobago wird die 'grosse karibische Erfolgsgeschichte' genannt and auch 'Wirtschaftlicher Tiger in einem Meer von Kätzchen'. Beides sind zutreffende Bechreibungen. Trinidad und Tobago steht an erster Stelle der karibischen Investitionstabellen, mit dem höhchsten per Kapita der direkten Auslandinvestitionen der gesamten weslichen Hemisphäre mit Ausnahme von Kanada. Niedrige Energiekosten, aufs Höchste geschulte und ausgebildete Arbeitskräfte, moderne Telekommunikation und Infrastruktur, und stabile demokratische Regierungen haben die Position von Trinidad und Tobago als den Handelsplatz der Karibik zementiert.

Die meisten der inländischen Investitionen beziehen sich haupttsächlich auf den Energiesektor, der 72% des Exports ausmacht. Die beträchtlichen Energiereserven wie Erdöl mit 0.84 Billionen Barrels und Erdgas mit 25.3 Trillionen Kubik Feet (ungefähr 8 Trillionen Kubikmeter) und steigend, haben Trinidad und Tobago zum industrialisiertesten Land der Karibik gemacht. Es ist der weltgrösste Exporteur für Ammoniak und ein Grosshersteller von Asphalt, Methanol, Karbamid und Stahl. Das Herzland der Industrie und Energie von Trinidad und Tobago ist Point Lisas. Dort liegt auch die grösste der Flüssigerdgas Anglage, die in diesem Teil der Hemisphäre jemals gebaut wurde.

Obgleich die Wirtschaft von Trinidad und Tobago in der Vergangenheit von Energie abhängig war, waren nachfolgende Regierungen durch schwankende Erdölpreise gezwungen die Wirtschaft abwechslungsreicher zu gestalten. Herstellungs- und Agrarsektor wurden erweitert so zum Beispiel die Lebensmittel-, Holz-, Verpackungs pharmazeutische-, Textil- und Bauindustrie und auch die Marineindustrie. Daraus ergaben sich der Aufbau weiterer Industrien wie Informatik, Finanzmarkt, Tourismus und Hotelindustrie, Umweltversorgung, Unterhaltungs- und Freizeitgestaltungsindustrie.

Vom strategischen Standpunkt her konnte Trinidad und Tobago nicht besser gelegen sein. Es liegt an den Handelskreuzstrassen der Amerikanischen Kontinente. Ideal um aus den sich erschliessenden grossen Handelsmärkten von Süd-, Mittel- und Nordamerika und der Karibik Nutzen zu ziehen. Das Land hat eine Reihe von fortlaufenden Handelsabkommen abgeschlossen mit den USA, Canada,

Grossbritannien, Frankreich, Brasilien, Argentinien, Spanien, dem Mittelamerikanischen Gemeinsamen Markt, der Karibischen Union (CARICOM) und dem Europäischen Gemeinsamen Markt (LOME IV).

Trinidad und Tobago's intensivierter Wirtschaftsmarkt, sein attraktives Investitionspaket und seine Anziehungskraft als die Zwillgsinsel, das Touristenparadies, werden von der regierungseigenen Wirtschaftsentwicklungsagentur "The Tourism und Industrial Development Company of Trinidad and Tobago" (TIDCO) aggresiv in Übersee angeboten. - www.tidco.co.tt

Tourismus ist die Haupteinnahmequelle von Tobago. Es ist eine der unverdorbendsten und schönsten Inseln der Karibik. Ihr Charme und Charakter sind noch kaum vom Massentourismus berührt; stattdessen hat sich Tobago auf den sensitiveren Ferienmarkt ausgerichtet, mit dem Ergebnis architektonisch geschmackvoller Gebäulichkeiten, die sich niedrig halten und der Umgebung angepassen sind. Im Jahre 2000 öffnete Trinidad und Tobago's grösstes touristen-orientiertes Projekt seine Türen: das 5-Sterne Tobago Plantagen Resort und Tobago Hilton in Lowlands. Der Touristenschwerpunkt der Insel liegt im Südwesten, um und herum Crown Point und den Internationalen Flughafen.

Auch in Trinidad schreitet der Tourismus schnell fort, dennoch, der Schwerpunkt ist auf Öko-Tourismus und Festlichkeiten der Karnivalzeit. Trinidad und Tobago's Hotel und Entwicklungs Akt will internationale Geschäftsleute anreizen hier zu investieren und bietet eine Unmenge von einladenden Anlageprämien und - vorteilen.

DIE EINZIGARTIGE NATURGESCHICHTE

Trinidad bietet den Naturliebhabern die Möglichkeit den südamerikanischen Regenwald zu geniessen ohne eigentlich dort hinzugehen. Als Trinidad vor langer Zeit vom südarmerikanischen Festland losgelöst wurde nahm es mit sich die Fauna und Flora. Diese Lage hat dazu geführt, dass Trinidad sich in seiner Naturgeschichte sehr wesentlich von den anderen Inseln der Karibik unterscheidet, das heisst, Trinidad kann sich rühmen eine Fauna und Flora gleich der karibischen Inselkette zu haben, aber auch der des südamerikanischen Kontinents.

Es gibt 433 Vogelarten in Trinidad, davon brüten 250 Vogelarten hier in Trinidad. Das 'Land des Kolibri' beheimatet 41 schillernde Arten des kleinen Vogelwunders. Des Asa Wright Naturgebiet an der nördlichen Bergkette ist eines der hervorragengsten Vogelgebieten der Welt. Tobago hat 13 Vogelarten, die man nicht in Trinidad findet.

Wildbestand von Trinidad

622 Schmetterlingarten, 108 Arten von Säugetieren, u.a. Rothaaraffe, Ozelot, Manatee, Armadillo, Baumstachelschwein, Peccarie, Wild, gigantische Lederschildkröten, die an der Nordküste Trinidad's brüten und in Tobago, 70 verschiedene Reptilienarten, 57 Fledermausarten, 2,700 verschiedener Arten von Büschen und Pflanzen, 700 Arten von Orchiden.

SEHENSWÜRDIGKEITEN UND WAS MAN SO UNTERNEHMEN KANN

TRINIDAD

The Queen's Park Savannah - zum 'liming' (ein typisch trinidadischer Ausdruck das etwa heisst wie sich mit seinen Freunden vergnüge und entspannen) - man geht spazieren, isst gekochten Mais und Austern, spielt Kricket, Rugby, geht zu Musikfestivals und zum Karnival. Westlich entlang der Savannah stehen die majestätischen Sieben, imposante alte Kolonial Herrschafshäuser, die jetzt anderweitig verwendet werden

Der botanische Garten

Queen's Park Oval ein berühmtes Kricket Stadium - Kricket ist der populärste Sport in der Karibik. Brian Lara, ein Trinidader ist einer der Kricket Sportgrössen und hat im Oval seine Karriere gemacht

Red House, das Parlamentsgebäude am Woodford Square

Brian Lara Promenade, der 'liming' Treffpunkt der Stadt

Frederick Street und Umgebung sind das Einkaufszentrum von Port of Spain

Chaguaramas - auf der nordwestlichen Halbinsel - Schauplatz der Miss Univers 1999

Chaguaramas National Park - wunderschöne beforstete Täler die eine grosse Anzahl von Wild beheimatet. Touren werden durch die Chaguaramas Development Authority (CDA) arrangiert

Marinas, Segeln, Fischen - da Chaguaramas ausserhalb des Hurrikangürtel liegt hat sich dort eine Marinedienstleistungsindustrie entwikelt mit modernen Marinas, geschmackvoll erbauten Restaurants und Geschäften entlang diesem lieblichen Küstenstreifen

Macqueripe Strand und Scotland Bucht

Chaguaramas öffentlicher Golfplatz mit einer 9-Löcher Anlage und schöner Umgebung

'Down the Islands' (dies sind kleine Inseln nahe der westlichen Halbinsel) isoliert und ruhig sind sie ein Ferien/Wochenendziel

NATURWUNDER
Nordküste und nördliche Bergkette- eine Gegend mit wunderschönen Stränden, und Gelegenheit zum Bergklettern und Vogelwacht (eine Liste der Öko-Touren, Hotels und Gästehäusern ist bei der Touristenagentur TIDCO erhältlich)

El Tucuche - der zweithöchste Berg der Insel (936 m) ein lohnender wenn auch ermüdender Aufstieg

Asa Wright Naturschutzgebiet auf der nördlichen Bergkette - bietet Touren, Unterkünfte und ein Studienzentrum an

Aripo Höhlen - grosser Höhlen Komplex, wo der blinde Ölvogel lebt

Caroni Sümpfe - geheimnisvolle Mangrovensümpfe eine halbe Stunde von Port of Spain entfernt, Heimat des Scarlet Ibis, der Nationalvogel von Trinidad und Tobago

Nariva Swamp - von grossem naturwissenschaftlichen Interesse in der Nähe von Manzanilla, ein Strand im Osten des Landes, Heimat der Affen, Anaconda, und Manatee

Gran Riviere, Matelot, Matura und Rincon an deren Strände die gigantichen Lederschildkröten ihre Eier legen

Pointe-a-Pierre Wildhuhn Park - ein Tierschutzgebiet auf einer ehemaligen Ölraffinerie Anlage

Pitch Lake - ein kaum merklich schäumender Asphalt See, den man begehen kann Sir Walter Raleigh benutzte diesen Asphalt, um seine Schiffe abzudichten. Der Asphalt wird ausgeführt und bedeckt Strassen von London bis New York

Devil's Woodyard - eine sonderliche geologische Erscheinung von Miniatur-Dreckvulkanen

Strände - an der idyllischen Nordküste: Maracas, Las Cuevas, Paria, Blanchisseuse, Matelot, Gran Riviere und Toco an der Nord-ostküste. An der Ostküste: Balandrabucht, Manzanilla und Mayaro, diese sind eingesäumt mit unzähligen Kokosbäumen, die dem wilden Atlantic trotzen. Im Südwesten liegen die Strände der Cedros Halbinsel.

ANDERE SEHENSWÜRDIGKEITEN
Mount St. Benedict Kloster - das älteste Benedektinerkloster in der Karibik. Von dort hat man einen herrlichen Blick auf das Flachland von Zentral-Trinidad

Angostura Brennerei - eine faszinierende Tour durch das Rum Geschäft und das berühmte Angostura Bitters

Waterloo Tempel - ein Hindu Tempel der von einer Person bei Hand mitten auf den Fluss gebaut wurde

San Fernando - Trinidad's zweite Stadt

SPORT
Kricket - Queen's Park Oval oder auf allen offenen Flächen

Golf - St. Andrews, Moka, nahe Port of Spain; Chaguaramas 9-Loch Anlage - öffentlicher Golfplatz; Pointe-a-Pierre Golf Klub, nahe Point Lisas

Fussball/Soccer - Hasley Crawford Stadium; Zentrun für Excellenz

Athlethischer Sport - Hasley Crawford Stadium

Tennis - Jean Pierre Komplex

Segeln und fischen - Chaguaramas und Nordküste

TOBAGO
Tauchen und schnorkeln - Tobago hat einige der sensationellsten Tauchmöglichkeiten in der Karibik. Die besten Plätze sind: Speyside, (wo man auch gigantischen Manta Rays schwimmen kann); Charlotteville und the Giles Inseln, beide an der Nordküste; Buccoo Riff und der grösste Teil der leewärts Küste, besonders Mt. Irvine, Amos Vale, Culloden Bucht und Castara

Öko-Tobago - das nördliche Waldgebiet, das älteste in der westlichen Hemisphere. Amos Vale und Klein Tobago für die Vogelwacht; Turtle Beach wo die gigantische Lederschildkröte ihre Eier legt; Argyll Wasserfall

Strände - alle Strände rund um Tobago sind wunderschön. Zu den schönsten zählen jedoch Pigeon Point und Store Bay nahe Crown Point; Mt. Irvine und Courland Bay sind weiter nörd lich; Castara, Englishman's Bay und Bloody Bay sind an der leewärtigen Küste; auf der luvseite der Küste, wo das Meer recht rauh ist, liegen Lowlands, Bacolet Bay, Fort Granby, und Speyside, was aber ruhige Wasser hat

Wassersport - am besten bei Pigeon Point, wo die Lagune perfect für Windsurfen und Wassersky ist

Fischen - Tobago's Gewässer sind voller Fisch. Eine der Höhepunkte des Sportfischen ist der jährliche Carib Beer Sportfisch-Wettbewerb zu Ostern

Golf - Mt. Irvine Bay Championship Golfplatz; der neue Jack Nicklaus Championship Golfplatz in den Tobago Plantagen in Lowlands

Ziegen - und Krebsrennen- in Buccoo, das Hauptquartier der Ziegen - und Krebsrennen. Siehe auch Rennwettbewerb mal anders jedes Osterwochenende

Scarborough - Fort King George auf einem Hügel gelegen mit atemberaubenden Blick über Küsten und Hauptstadt; das Tobago Museum, in dem Barracken-Wachthaus von Fort King George, erzählt die blutige Geschichte der Insel; der botanische Garten